CROSS COUNTRY RUNNING

CROSS COUNTRY RUNNING

Marc Bloom

© 1978 by
World Publications
P.O. Box 366, Mountain View, CA 94042

*No information in this book may be reprinted in
any form without permission from the publisher*

Library of Congress #77-84523
ISBN 0-89037-0915 (Hb) -092-3 (Pb)

Dedication to Andrea
and
Allison

Foreword

Matters of running have consumed more of my life than anything else since I was "the fastest kid on the block" as a pre-teen in the late 1950s. I memorized the 1960 world records, long since forgotten, and later pursued running journalism, of which this book is my most ambitious single effort.

But my sensitivity to—and understanding of—running was far from advanced until I started running myself. I did run in high school, and while that experience was very important to me, I imbibed things that had to be unlearned when I began jogging in the spring of 1972. Occasional jogging led to devoted running and an addiction to daily exercise. My health and well-being have improved a great deal, and I hope I have become a better person because of it.

My personal experiences in running have helped me in my professional pursuits, in my contact with other runners and my writings about them. My perceptions of athletic life, I think, have likewise improved.

When I ran cross-country in high school, I never thought I would ever return to it—much less give it so much time. But even in 1962, when I first saw the famous Van Cortlandt Park course in the Bronx, I sensed there was something special going on there, something that was meaningful to runners if not totally satisfying.

This book has its roots in *The Harrier*, a cross-country publication I started in 1974. As the sport was bared before me, and I recognized its strengths and weaknesses, its history, its application in the United States and elsewhere, I decided there was indeed a rich, factual account that needed to be told. I have tried to write about the most significant aspects of cross-country running in order to provide a broad, overall picture of where it has been, what is happening to it now and where it is headed.

By and large, I like what I see. The more of us who discover the joys of running, the more will gravitate to and support cross-country. If this book contributes to that, I will be forever gratified.

Marc Bloom
Staten Island, N.Y.
August 1977

Acknowledgements

I wish to thank the following persons for their assistance in providing information for this book. Alphabetically, they are:

Doug Andersen, cross-country coach, Westville High School, Natal, South Africa; Larry Bortstein, free-lance writer; Edward J. J. Bowes, track and cross-country coach, Bishop Loughlin High School, Brooklyn, N.Y.; Larry Byrne, IC4A Officials Association; Keith Caywood, coordinator of athletics, Kansas State Teachers College, Emporia, Kansas.

Peter Diamond, *Track & Field News;* Joe Fox, director of track and field and cross-country for the Catholic High Schools Athletic Association of New York City; Dr. Seymour Mac Goldstein; V. Goyers, General Secretary, Royal Belgium Athletic Association; Bob Hersh, *Track & Field News.*

Hal Higdon, Editor-at-Large, *Runner's World*; Lothar Hirsch, National Long-Distance Coach, German Athletic Federation; John B. Holt, Secretary, International Amateur Athletics Federation; Walt Krolman, assistant track and cross-country coach; St. John's University, New York; Martin Lewis, director of track and field and cross-country for the Public Schools Athletic League of New York City; James O'Neill, public relations director of the Hong Kong Marathon.

I would also like to express my gratitude to James O. Dunaway, William J. Miller and Professor Irving Rosenthal for their longtime professional and personal guidance.

M.B.

Contents

Part One:
ROOTS

1
The Natural Sport

We Americans love to label things. It gives us great satisfaction. We do it to people and governments and philosophies and lifestyles. In every field of human endeavor, there is a special jargon, and part of that jargon includes arbitrary labels. This is done sometimes for political purposes, other times for identification and convenience, for it is much easier to consider something by its label than to be analytical about it.

For years, runners remained aloof from the labeling game. Nobody called us anything. (I am not counting the unfortunate souls who yelled—and still yell—obscenities to passing runners from their car windows.) Nobody called us anything, because there just weren't enough of us to matter.

We are a people that thrives on numbers, because our economy is structured that way. If millions of us suddenly abandoned the tennis courts and bowling alleys and started, say, to shoot marbles for exercise, therapy and sexual fulfillment, we would constitute a significant phenomenon. In addition to the behavioral scientists trying to figure out what the hell had happened, marbleists would be on the covers of

Time and *Newsweek,* there would be a best-seller entitled *The Compleat Marbler,* and MGM would have on its hands a smash-hit about a gay marble champion portrayed by Dustin Hoffman. Jackie Onassis would appear on opening night.

When the running wave curled from coast to coast, we runners started to matter, because someone had to supply 10 million (at last count) runners with shoes and accessories with which to fuel our passion. We saw ourselves on the covers of national magazines, and fitness finally became socially acceptable.

But that also put us into The Label Game. Are you a "jogger" or a "runner"? Who cares? Lots of us. It was not enough that upon leaving the office we scurried into the bathroom like Clark Kent in a phone booth and changed from teacher or accountant or writer or attorney to a fitness freak. What are you anyway, jogger or runner? (Well, both of them beat my phrasing—"fitness freak.") This debate grew into an issue, and runners and joggers addressed themselves to it in *Runner's World* magazine.

Personally, I'd rather be called a "runner." Okay, I admit it. The term "jogger" conjures an image—to non-runners if not to ourselves—of an overweight guy overdressed in a heavy sweatsuit, dripping wet from a snail's-pace mile or two on a Sunday morning. He wears basketball sneakers. That is usually the dividing line: basketball sneakers.

Whenever I encounter a new face on my running turf, I tend to glance quickly at his feet. If he is wearing official, honest-to-goodness running shoes, then, by golly, he is an official, honest-to-goodness runner. Why else would he have invested $30? Yes, maybe it is to be chic or fashionable, but that tendency is not really as prevalent as we like to think. If he is wearing basketball sneakers, I figure he must get high on basketball, which is a marvelous sport, and is putting in a few miles to improve his stamina and thereby help his game. Boy, do I hate to get outrun during a workout by a guy in basketball sneakers!

So I tell those who inquire that I am a runner, but that my moderate pace would be considered jogging by the champions. One must get into relative terms here. The more I think about it, though, the more ridiculous it seems. I have always considered it quite virtuous for one to lead one's life free of the bonds of conformity, of which labelmania is a part. I think I have succeeded in living this way, so I am tempted to ignore the whole matter of runner vs. jogger. It is easier for the champions to do this. Their achievements are recognized. Marginal athletes such as myself are either too presumptuous of their skill or too insecure in what they are doing. I plead guilty on both counts.

The New York Times does an amusing thing with labels. It carries a "Sports Today" listing of daily events in the circulation area. This is setup in alphabetical order, with baseball at the top and track at the bottom. (That's track as in track and field.) Into this category goes anything at all that involves running. A 30-kilometer road race in Central Park, sponsored by the New York Road Runner's Club, will be called "Track."

I have thought about calling this to the attention of one of the assistant sports editors, especially since I know people there. But the journalist in me reacted, and I understand *The Times'* treatment. Its readership also identifies any form of running as "track" (maybe *because* of *The Times'* treatment?) and refers to someone like Frank Shorter as a "track star." Besides, *The Times'* editors, with all their wisdom and experience, probably would not know when a certain type of running event should be designated not as track, or even as road running, but as cross-country. So I will help them.

The term "cross-country," which originated in late-19th. century England, is a misnomer if one attempts to consider it literally. Runners do not run across an entire country—not all at once, anyway. Bruce Tulloh and a few others have actually taken a couple of months to run—30 or 40 miles a day—from America's West Coast to its East Coast, or vice versa. Those usually have been solo efforts with the adventurers racing only against themselves, trying to repress a breakdown in will and a cornucopia of blisters.

Runners are constantly seeking new worlds to conquer, both in training and in competition. It was not enough just to run marathons, so we have ultra-marathons. It was not enough to run them on flat surfaces, so we run them up and down steep hills. It was not enough to run hard and be done with it, so we run hard, rest and repeat the process for a full 24 hours. And so on.

Running is our food, and our hunger is never satisfied. We seek the ultimate, if not for ourselves then for others stronger than we. In the immediate future, the ultimate may be a revival of the trans-America race as run in the 1920s. I won't be in it, but I will savor it just the same—and I will write about it, I hope, with the same zeal and passion that will propel the participants to the completion of their journey.

We aren't talking about this kind of cross-country running here. Nevertheless, the term does make sense because the "country" part of it is merely a shortened version of countryside, across which Englishmen in particular would race a hundred years ago. To this day, the seman-

4

tics have not changed. Cityfolk go out or up or down "to the country" for their vacations, to the rural, spacious countryside that is embroidered with peace and quiet.

Now that our framework is in order, we can best determine exactly what cross-country is—by finding out what it is not. It is not track running or road running, the two other most popular forms of running in the US today. Thus, in a sense, it is everything else. Cross-country is running not done around an engineered track or on engineered roads. It is done everywhere else.

Cross-country makes use of our natural resources—which, sadly, are diminishing all around us. It brings the runner closer to nature, to God's gift of things green and fragrant and pristine—without artificial preservatives. It takes the legs of man and woman churning over the land, not the bypasses, becoming ever more sensitive to and sanitized from the environment.

You are running cross-country if you are doing that—if you are spurning the precision and predictability and symmetry of a quarter-mile track, or if you are avoiding the convenience and comfort of a carefully marked road. I do not wish to place a value on the kind of venue where one chooses to run. That is immature and self-defeating. But let us know where we are, exactly, when we run. Let us separate the authentic from the imitation, because to do so will cultivate our senses and heighten our experience.

There was a time when these natural resources were in abundance, and all one had to do to join them was step out the front door. Now, in the United States and other industrial nations, this wonderland is not quite as plentiful. Many of us, especially in the urban centers, must seek out the countryside for the natural terrain that will enable us to run cross-country.

When I step out my front door, there are many running options, none of which fits into the province of cross-country. I live on Staten Island, New York City's "fifth borough," a suburban enclave connected to the mainland by the Verrazano Bridge. My running companion, James Behr, and I enjoy working out along the hilly roads. But we frequently lament a pattern that prevents us from running cross-country, from enjoying our workouts a good deal more.

Millions of trees disappear as though victims of robbers in the night, uprooted by bulldozers clearing mini-forests for real estate developers. The dirt roads are gone, and the ones left, in the semi-rural sections, are guarded by junkyard dogs whose howls can be heard for several furlongs. When homes are built and roads are paved, with them come more cars and people and dogs and delivery trucks and donut palaces—all well and good, but tough on us runners who contend that the best things in life are green.

For natural running, I can either drive 10 minutes to the nearest park or run to a nearby golf course. It is perhaps ironic that golf courses have become one of the symbols of American cross-country running. Golf courses are hardly natural phenomena. They usually *replace* natural phenomena. We sometimes confuse them with the natural state of things because they are so pretty. We associate beauty with nature, forgetting how skilled we can be at producing pluperfect replicas of nature.

To run on a golf course is to run cross-country, even though such terrain is a contrivance of sorts. We must consider these places in terms of our culture. Just as our language changes and we accept altered usage, our land changes and as runners we must accept that. We may not like it, but we must adjust to it.

There is another irony here: I would wager that the vast majority of runners who has ever dotted the expanse of a golf course has never golfed. Time is essential. Serious runners would never give up a workout in favor of a round of golf, and since a round of golf consumes the better part of a nice day, when would one also run? Moreover, runners are "doers," and there seems to be very little doing in golf.

There are some places left in this country where golf courses are either not to be found or are off-limits to the straying runner. And not everyone lives in close proximity of wooded trails or municipal parks. That is hardly the end-all of cross-country.

Natural terrain, the foundation of cross-country, varies from locale to locale just as the dialects and mores do. The beaches and the coastline, the pastures and the forests, the deserts and the mountains, at high and low altitude. America's landscape is a potpourri of running opportunity. To probe this, we must become unsynchronized, indeed unreliant on the assurances of time and distance.

At times, it is appropriate to hedge further on my definition of cross-country and make it more encompassing. For one reason or another, there are many cross-country events that put runners partially on paved roads. What flanks these roads—dense greenery—may be the essence of cross-country. But, again, there is the concrete turnoff.

Here, realism must nudge idealism, and I offer a compromise: cross-country events that take in paved roads will not be smeared if they are generally off-limits to automobiles. (This gesture would never be permitted by the Europeans, especially the British, who thrive not only on natural terrain but on natural obstacles that make cross-country racing a thoroughly exhausting, yet memorable experience.)

Thus, cross-country is a type of natural running. The land is shared when one runs through it, and it is a privilege to have done so. Let us not abandon or abuse it while the supply lasts.

2
Its Beginnings

Cross-country running may be as old as civilized man, since many thousands of years ago athletic contestants had only the natural environment at their disposal. The crudest forms of footracing, dating back to early civilizations, have been documented by historians. The classics tell of the emphasis placed on sport and games by the Greeks. And there are legends of incredible running feats over brutal terrain that are embellished at opportune times, when we are most vulnerable and anxious to swallow the tales of the ancient marathoner.

Yet it was not until the 19th century that cross-country began to gain a shape and structure. This was the period of infancy of organized athletics in general, and cross-country clearly had its place. In fact, there is an interesting historical parallel between the development of cross-country in England and of baseball in America. Both sports existed in rudimentary form in the late 1800s and acquired widespread prominence just before the turn of the century, when the Modern Olympic Games and the Major Leagues were established.

American cross-country has its roots in the countryside of Great Britain. English writers Montague Shearman and F.A.M. Webster hold the last word on this matter. In his book *Athletes and Football*, published in 1887, Shearman included a section written by Walter Rye, president of the Thames Hounds and Hares Club. The subject: "Paper-Chasing and Cross-Country." Rye, a Victorian gentleman, used his own athletic experiences to document the origins of modern cross-country.

"At the end of 1867, a few members (of whom the writer was one) of the Thames Rowing Club at Putney conceived the idea of holding some cross-country steeplechases during the winter season, with the idea of keeping themselves more or less in condition until rowing began again. As may well be imagined, the arrangements of Thames Handicap Steeplechase Number One, as it was called, were primitive in the extreme, and indeed, the whole affair was treated more as a joke than anything else."

Rye tells of the race: "The competitors were taken up to the starting place on Wimbleton Common—the edge of Beverly Brook by the bridge—in a bus and had to dress how they could, and the race was run in the dark over about 2-1/4 miles of the roughest and boggiest part of the Common, then very difficult indeed as to its surface. Still, there were a dozen starters out of 20 entries, and the affair being the first cross-country steeplechase (not being at a school) that had ever taken place, attracted much attention in the athletic world."

Rye's non-school reference to this "first" cross-country event emphasizes the weight given to club activities in Britain even then and implicitly states that school cross-country had an earlier birth.

Webster knew Walter Rye personally and hailed him as the "Father of Paper-Chasing," in light of Rye being the founder of the pioneering Thames Hounds and Hare Club. Paper-chasing referred to the marking of a cross-country route. The flag system was not in effect then. Prior to the race, a couple of runners would set out as "hares," with a sausage-shaped canvas bag of paper strips to be laid as trails for the pack of "hounds" to follow. A handful of this paper—bookbinders' cuttings 6-8 inches long—would be dropped every 20 yards or so. The hares were clever artisans of deception and took pleasure in obfuscating the plight of the hounds.

Rye wrote, "Whenever the country gives an opportunity, a 'false' scent should be laid, e.g. at crossroads. An artful hare will often drop his 'false' faintly only and lay his real scent strong and clear, most of the hounds rushing to the conclusion that he is trying to take them in, and that it is very unlikely that he would, when the scents bifurcate, give a good one on a real track. One hare will often take a false straight up a ploughed field over the brow of the hill so that it is impossible for the hounds to see its cessation without following it to the bitter end."

An advance notice of a paper-chase appeared in a publication called *The Sportsman* on Oct. 3, 1868. It read, "A handicap paper hunt will take place on Saturday, 17th October, starting from the King's Head, Roehampton Bottom at 4:30 p.m. Hounds, who must be introduced by some member of the Thames Rowing Club or belong to an athletic club, rowing club, school, etc., will be roughly handicapped. A pewter will be given to the hound first to reach the hare."

The public schools, however, were the forerunners, literally, of the clubs. Webster, in his 1929 *Athletics of Today*, tells of the Crick Run at Rugby in 1837 and cross-country events at Shrewsbury at an even earlier date, although he does not give an exact beginning. It became a Shrewsbury custom to hold weekly runs during the Christmas semester. These events were more like survival training than athletic contests.

Webster describes it: "The 'Gentleman of the Run,' who formed the first division of the pack, ran coatless and carried a short bludgeon as a defense weapon against the town toughs, who took a delight in stoning the boys. Latterly, the gentleman's bludgeon became the record of his prowess. It was ringed in years and a notch cut for each run. The notch was replaced with a cross to mark a win or 'kill,' and a square bracket substituted to denote a second place."

So, while legendary American gunslingers were carving notches in their pistols after sundown duels on the Western prairie, British harriers duly enriched the history of their country by racing through an onslaught of headhunters, defending their honor and their achilles tendons and—who knows?—the girl back home. Why was this not depicted in *The Loneliness of the Long-Distance Runner?*

Webster goes on: "The second division, or hounds, used to run in jackets and mortar-boards, from which every atom of stiffening material had been removed. Anything up to 130 couples of hounds would start in an ordinary run, but for the longer distances, varying from 9-12 miles, six or eight picked 'couples' only were allowed to start. The first half-dozen boys home were allowed a hot supper at the shop, at the club's expense. These runs culminate in senior and junior steeplechases over very stiff Shropshire country, and the boys are equipped with hedging gloves sewn to the sleeves of their jerseys.

"At Rugby, where the course crosses water where the Clifton Brook runs slow and muddy down a sheltered green valley to meet Avon, water jumps and a few stiff-set hedges supply the obstacles, and at Bradfield the course follows the valley of the Ring, and the finish is made through about 15 feet of deep water in a trout pool, while at Sedburgh the run is over all of 10-12 miles of real hill country."

These were school kids, remember—teenagers. This went a bit farther than what now is asked by our President's Commission on Physical Fitness. The early English runs almost sound like a bad day at boot camp in the Marine Corps.

The Thames Club was joined by several others with names like South London Harriers, Birchfield Harriers (The New York Yankees of their day), Spartan Harriers and Mosely Harriers. The harrier label obviously stems from the hares of the paper-chase, and it is still used commonly today—in America as well as in England—as a reference to cross-country runners.

Thereafter, despite Rye's lament of the "evils" of recruiting (i.e., importing runners for club benefits), and course restrictions (to enable "gate" money) confronting cross-country, the sport gained enormous momentum. In 1876, Britain held its first national championship, an event that maintains great prestige today. It was run through the wilds of Epping Forest, and in the best tradition of distance running, everyone reportedly got lost. Why they got lost the historians do not reveal, except to imply that the runners themselves were at fault, having been victimized by the "wilds" of the route. The following year, the course was carefully planned and no one, so they say, went astray.

Oxford and Cambridge soon got into the act, and British cross-country leaped unabated into the 20th century, cultivating its depth and success, and spreading its good fortune far beyond its borders.

The earliest date found for organized cross-country in America is 1890 when the Amateur Athletic Union (founded in 1888) conducted a championship event. The race was won by W.D. Day of the New Jersey Athletic Club. The Prospect Harriers of Brooklyn captured the team title. It is difficult not to conclude that the Prospect Harriers were named after Brooklyn's Prospect Park, which is a marvelous site for cross-country running today—if one can avoid those bent on crime who lurk there after darkness falls.

From 1899-1907, college cross-country in the United States was looked after by the Intercollegiate Cross-Country Association of America. In 1908, control over it was acquired by what is known today as the IC4A—the Intercollegiate Amateur Athletic Association of America. That year, Cornell won the first of four straight titles, and the school's H.C. Young won the gold medal.

Meanwhile, France, Belgium, Finland and a few other countries had also adopted the sport, and the first International Championship was

11

held (appropriately, in England) in 1903. The US did not enter the International in the meet's early years, for participation was confined to member nations of the International Cross-Country Union.

The US became a factor on the international level in the Olympics, which patronized cross-country only in 1912, '20 and '24. Cross-country remains in the Olympics only as part of the modern pentathlon, which is a bit ironic since in the first Greek Olympics, in 776 B.C., there was a footrace in a meadow beside the river Alpheus. This definitely qualifies as cross-country.

Herbert Warren Wind wrote in *The Realm of Sport*, "Coroebus, the winner, was crowned with a wreath of wild olive, a garland woven from the twigs and leaves of the tree that Hercules—so sang the ancient poets—had sought in the lands of Hyperboreans and planted in the sacred grove near the temple of Zeus at Olympia."

Almost 2700 years later, on Sunday, Dec. 8, 1907, a banner headline on the front page of *The New York Times* sports section blared: "Big and Little Stars of the Popular Cross-Country Sport Now at Height of Its (sic) Season." Apparently, the craft of succinct headline writing was not yet advanced, nor were professional sports which grew to supplant cross-country and other amateur athletics in cultural impact.

The story that accompanied the headline stated: "There is perhaps no branch of sport that has in it the widely beneficial elements that cross-country running has. Although it is a comparatively new game in America, it has acquired about New York alone a tremendous following. There are fully 500 athletes engaged in New York cross-country running in the fall and spring seasons, and half that number run throughout the winter. All of these are not competitors in contests but run for the value of vigorous exercise. It is a sport that deserves wider popularity than it has, and it promises to grow until it becomes one of the major sports of the nation.

"One of its greatest attractions lies in the fact that it is absolutely free. There is no possibility of gain connected with it. It cannot be connected with gate receipts and can have no awards to prompt any suggestion or taint of professionalism. As a spectacle, it attracts along the courses used as many as 50,000 people...."

The Times was a bit shortsighted, for cross-country's "attraction" in not deflowering its financial virginity is exactly what lessened its stature, as major league baseball and college football emerged. Babe Ruth and Knute Rockne are a tough act to follow. But on New Year's Day 1908, the article went on to explain, a Grand American Cross-Country Handicap would be held in American Legion Park in Washington Heights. High school runners would compete at three miles, older men at 6-1/2 miles.

Cross-country continued to increase in popularity as coaches and distance runners came to rely on it then as valuable conditioning for the track seasons. The AAU sponsored many events, including its national championship. College conference activity was initiated, and the National Collegiate Athletic Association (NCAA) staged its first national meet in 1938.

Interest naturally filtered into the school programs, and high schools in New York City conducted events as early as 1907. The growth of cross-country began to match the growth of track and field, although cross-country—then and now—is not in the same league with track as a generator of public interest. Cross-country was considered by many as an inferior arm of track, not as an independent sport worthy of merit in its own right.

Almost a year to the day after it hailed the increasing interest in cross-country, *The Times* gave conspicuous play to one of the first high school events. On Dec. 5, 1908, the New York City public schools race was the lead sports story. Three pictures accompanied the article, which started off:

"Facing a cold, penetrating wind, 55 long-distance runners yesterday competed in the high school cross-country championship, which was held near Celtic Park, Long Island City, under the auspices of the PSAL. For the contestants, it was an ideal day, but the delay at the start caused by the dilatoriousness of the Commerce High School team chilled many of the runners and stiffened their limbs. . . . It was a real cross-country course except minus the water jump. The path was across several hills, rough edges and stony, uneven patches of ground covered here and there by piles of gravel and tangled masses of shrubbery."

The 3-1/2 mile course was the same one used for the AAU events. The race was won by C. Major of Boys High, who defeated O. DeGrouchy of Erasmus Hall by 100 yards. Eight full teams took part, and DeWitt Clinton was the victor.

In deference to the ruggedness of cross-country, it was considered primarily a foul-weather activity, frequently associated with the harshness of the elements. Years ago, it was almost the exclusive property of the Midwest and Northeast, where the miseries of adverse weather are regularly inflicted on athletic contests.

In the East, the collegians had the IC4A to look after them. In the Midwest, the Big Ten held its first conference race in 1919, and it was won by Wisconsin. The start of the University of Illinois program dates back to 1905, and Eastern Michigan, to cite one more example, started cross-country in 1911. Army and Navy first met in 1937. Navy won.

Today, cross-country in America is more than a sport; just like running in general, it has become a lifestyle. The bustling school programs, for boys *and* girls, corner most of the competition and are confined to the fall months. There is some overlap into the road running sphere, which includes a small percentage of pure cross-country events sprinkled throughout the year.

Fitness lovers—and they are that: in love with being fit—are running off the beaten paths, into the territory of cross-country. It is happening in varied forms all over the world and is a far cry from the paper-chasing Britons of 1867.

In 1967, the Thames Hare and Hounds Club held a paper chase to commemorate its centennial. When the club members met, they no doubt exchanged stories passed on about canvas shoes and flannel knickerbockers and steeplechase jumps, of the 24-mile run around several villages won by one J. Scott in a little over three hours. To further celebrate their forefathers' contributions, they must have bathed in a lukewarm tub after their run, downed steaming glasses of port negus and capped the evening meal with ginger beer and song.

No, not everything about cross-country running has changed in the last hundred years.

3
Its Aesthetic Appeal

I spend a good deal of time in a New York City junior high school, teaching reluctant 14-year-old students how to write better than they think they can. One writing assignment that is always a big hit is, "My Last Day on Earth."

There is an unfortunate morbid tone to it, especially for those of us who cannot even recall being 14. But these teenagers do not interpret the topic to be ominous; 14-year-olds consider themselves immortal. They write not of old age or disease but of some scientific phenomenon that will thrust the earth into the solar systems beyond.

And what will they do on the very last day? Buy mopeds, eat pizza, cut school—and a few unmentionables. Then, as they sometimes do, they smile with premature incredulity and pose the thought to me.

I tell them this: If I was of sound mind and body, I would find the nearest large wooded area and run for two hours or so on rolling dirt roads. I would want it to be early autumn, when it would still be warm enough to sweat and the leaves would be a mesh of colors, and my company would be the squirrels and the rabbits. My path would be narrow, and a bit winding and hilly. The trees would flank me high

15

overhead, sloping toward a morning sun that would peek between the tallest branches. Afterward, I would be ready to get my affairs in order and await my destiny.

They laugh at that. And my story affirms for them the notion that teachers are crazy anyway and wouldn't know how to have a good time if it was staring them in the face.

Ivan Doig knows how to enjoy himself. Writing in *The New York Times* Sunday travel section, he tells of his running vacations:

"So far, my on-the-road running has been from sea level to 7000 feet, urban lakeside to high chaparrel country, alone in the dawn amid thundering herds of hoofers. I can report that jogging while traveling takes surprisingly little extra effort. Also that, done with a bit of discrimination and a few minutes invested over the map of an unfamiliar place to discern its fancier sites for footwork, the daily jog can become a travel adventure in its own right.

"Where to run? Consider shorelines of whatever sort. Lakes, rivers, bays, harbors, canals—all are reasonable bets for scenery-to-jog-by. Public parks are a natural, but some boast more on-foot allure than others. Look to those with grand vista, such as Montreal's Mont Royale Park high over the city or San Francisco's green and undulant Golden Gate Park. Or those with bonuses such as marked jogging paths or a *Parcours*, the Swiss-devised 'fitness trail' with basic exercise apparatus—for situps, chinups and similar exertions—along the route."

Doig runs at a moderate pace, as most of us do, but even the champions with their reliance on track speed, speak well of the favors of natural cross-country running. Ron Daws, a 1968 US Olympian in the marathon (placing 22nd in Mexico City), tells "how it began" for him years earlier in his autobiography, *The Self-Made Olympian:*

"I often roamed the great bird sanctuaries, lake shores and wooded parks, letting my imaginations construct vivid pictures of what it would be like to run effortlessly through the woods," writes the Minneapolis native. "Finally, while wandering one of the trails in a wooded preserve one afternoon when I was 12, visions of the past when frontiersmen ran to elude pursuers came over me. Springy pine needles and dry leaves carpeted the path until it curved out of sight and distant trees waited in the half-light.

"Swept up in the imagery, I could no longer resist the urge to run. I raced away at full tilt. It was a dream come true. Great strides carried me up and down easy hills. One crisp autumn breeze was charged with the scent of pines and in filling my lungs seemed to propel me onward...."

Daws' competitive initiation brought forth some mediocre miling: "I would have quit running then, except I noticed one salient difference between racing and other sports. If, for instance, after practice my swat at a baseball missed by only three inches instead of four, the result of the game was precisely the same. But in running, even minute improvement could be detected by the watch, and there was a lot of room for improvement. This was the first concrete encouragement I'd received at a sport, and I began to look forward to the cross-country season which, without confining stadiums and tracks, would be more akin to my initial concept of free running. Cross-country captured my heart."

Daws' book shows pictures of him running at 9000 feet elevation in the Colorado Rockies, in a Minnesota park, through the Badlands of South Dakota and barefoot in a 1960 cross-country race.

Ivan Doig, who lives in Seattle, is one of an increasing number of urbanites escaping to more enraptured surroundings via vacation cross-country running. I am another one. So is John Roemer, who told in *Runner's World* of his running on part of the Appalachian Trail. The Trail spans 2000 miles from Maine to Georgia. Roemer concentrated on the 37 miles of it that pass through Maryland. He wrote:

"It's a runner's delight—except for a mile or two of very rocky terrain." Roemer's trip took him through winding, forested mountain roads, on narrow dirt paths, over broad, grassy stretches, atop scenic overlooks, up and down stony passages and into a "jungle" of briars and bushes.

"You'll pick up a few souvenirs among the thorns and you'll probably hallucinate about lurking pythons," he said. But "you're evidently safe in Maryland. I run in the woods every day in a state park in northern Maryland, and I've seen only one snake in five years, a harmless black racer who didn't even look up when I jumped over him."

George Young, who has been on the Olympic team four times—a feat no other US distance runner has accomplished—is more of a snake expert. Young, who now coaches at Central Arizona Junior College, spent his mornings—every morning—in cross-country runs through the Arizona desert.

"There's not much prettier sights," said George. "It makes you wonder why everybody doesn't get up at 6 o'clock just to watch the sunrise."

Young was not the only one watching the sunrise and sidestepping the cacti on those desert outings. There were coyotes and lizards and,

17

above all, rattlesnakes.

"From early May through the summer, and even possibly into November, you can depend on running across quite a few rattlesnakes," Young said in his biography, *Always Young*, written with Philadelphia sports columnist Frank Dolson.

"It's really funny. You're running along, thinking about running races, your heart's beating pretty fast, and you're working up a sweat. But when that rattlesnake rattles, your heart will sure increase the stroke for a few minutes. It's really upsetting for a little while after, because it completely destroys your concentration. You're going along, you've got a good, hard pace going—I might be mentally running a race against somebody—and then you hear this sound. You jump two or three times. Then you stop, you go back, and you might kill him with a rock or stick or something, or you might leave him alone. Then you spend the rest of the time tip-toeing along looking for another rattlesnake."

Once, I encountered a snake while running. It was about a mile from my Staten Island, N.Y., home, and it was curling onto a semi-paved road from the bushes of a wooded area when I spotted it. It was a harmless garter snake, but I took pleasure in telling others of this meeting, for it gave me a sense of adventure, as though I were an explorer upon primitive ground.

Recently, my running partner, Jimmy Behr, and I have come across turtles. Our *modus operandi* is to stop running and try to coax the turtle off the road, where it is certain to be smashed by traffic. Once, when we got close to one, its neck extended and it snapped at us. We noticed its large feet and long tail. Soon, our coaxing was unnecessary. The turtle moved quickly from the road to the bordering brush. To us, this was no turtle—at least no species with which we were familiar. We joked that perhaps it had escaped from the Staten Island Zoo, and we would be subject to arrest for aiding and abetting a delinquent reptile.

I have also seen rabbits and quail scatter in the side woods. Now, I see them less frequently. Occasionally, I see a rabbit splattered on the road, for that once semi-paved road is now a fully-paved road, making it easier for cars to speed the sharp, blind turns. Other dirt roads within an hour's run of my home have been coated with concrete and tar. The natural clusters of trees and woods, indigenous to Staten Island as to no other part of New York City, have been raped by bulldozers. So I anticipate with great desire my annual summer vacation, when I can escape to places that are green and pretty and fragrant, to look around, take pictures and, of course, run.

My most memorable running excursions in cross-country territory were in 1972, in the Northwest, and 1973, in the Border South. In 1972, my wife, Andrea, and I flew to Salt Lake City, rented a car and touched bases in several national parks in the US and Canadian Rockies. The following year, with our six-month-old Allison, we hit much of scenic North Carolina, Tennessee and Virginia.

Some of my running was done on paved roads like highway shoulders; the adventure in me was not yet kindled, and I often opted for the path nearest our motel. Besides, family obligations, not running, had to be my first priority, and that was quite bloated with sightseeing and care for our child. Yet, I was able to stray off the main arteries now and then, and I have retained vivid recollections of those experiences.

We were bunked in a cabin in Yellowstone National Park, not far from Yellowstone Lake. The altitude there is something above 8000 feet, similar to the elevation in Mexico City where 1968 Olympic distance runners were victimized by the "thin" air. I ran on paths around the lake and tried to devour the fresh mountain air. But I could not. It was a strange sensation, as though the more I inhaled the more fleeting the air and the more evasive the taste. I felt a stinging in my chest and was prematurely short of wind. Running in those surroundings, one wants to feel everything, but the rarified air is like a guardian of the land, warning the newcomer that he must first be initiated and then adapt to its demands.

There were similar outings amid the Grand Tetons in Wyoming, in Glacier National Park in Montana and into Canada's Banff and Jasper Parks. The magnificent Rockies—can those who live in their midst ever take them for granted?—formed an imposing backdrop to my running.

In the Tetons, I was running up a narrow incline flanked by dense wooded patches when a deer surprised me. It headed toward me. I ran for cover, but it turned out that the deer had gazed beyond me and had something else in mind. It made no move in my direction and faded into the camouflaging landscape.

Glacier Park, located in northwestern Montana, is my favorite place in the United States. It seemed distinguished from other national parks in that commercialism, at least then, had not at all penetrated its primitiveness. The few shops and eateries that I saw did not detract from the natural beauty.

We were lodged near Lake MacDonald, and our first night there a storm whipped through the area. The picture-postcard lake became ruffled in disarray, its waters pulling in vain to settle down. The setting took on a very remote air, evoking in me a heightened desire to run and get high on the wilderness at hand.

The next day dawned clear. I arbitrarily selected my route, a mess of a road through which no car going at an excessive speed could avoid mishap. I saw no cars. I heard sounds of movements in the adjacent woods, sounds of silence, if you will, sounds that scared me. I am chicken when confronted with the unknown—although there is something in me, I think, that wants to confront it.

The sounds that followed my run drew thoughts of angry wildlife descending upon me. What would I do, I pondered, if a bear came charging out of the woods, as they are known to do in these places? I made it to the end of the path where I found a quaint general store, to which I later returned with my wife. I ran back on the same path, completing an hour's journey.

Two days later, we got word that snow had fallen in the higher elevations during the night and blocked passage on some obscure roads leading out of the park. It was August. The thought of snow in August further intrigued me, and I set out to see it for myself while running. I found hiking trails near a ranger station and ran into the snow, which was partially melted from the morning sun. I reveled in it. People walked about in sandals and shorts—and ski parkas. Andrea finally caught up with me and snapped some pictures.

Two runs in Canada highlight my memories. One took me on dirt roads from our modest accommodations to the exquisite Jasper Park Lodge, where we were to go boating and cycling and have lunch. The other, in Vancouver, took me along the surf and into sections of Stanley Park, the largest municipal park in North America.

The following summer, we planned on hitting four main destinations: Shenandoah Park and the Blue Ridge Mountains; Smoky Mountains Park; Cape Hatteras and the Outer Banks, and Colonial Williamsburg.

A country club golf course beckoned me in Pennsylvania, en route to our first landmark. It was a meticulously manicured amalgam of greens and fairways and, at the dinner hour on a humid evening, the course was studded with the flow of waving sprinklers. The people having cocktails on the patio could see me move from one knoll to the next and were more amused than irked by my presence. My periodic rinsing through the wall of sprayed water at each hole was fully intended, and the few golfers motorcarting around smiled ingenuously. After an hour, I was delightfully drenched. But I paid for my fun with a cold that sidelined me for the next two days.

The Outer Banks neck into the Atlantic from the North Carolina mainland and the Cape Hatteras seashore there has some of the biggest waves on the East Coast. This is the place that often braces for late-summer hurricanes that charge up from the Caribbean.

I got rid of my socks and shoes, and for the first time ran barefoot. I ran along the beach, edging around the crashing surf and catching the eyes of sunbathers. What a liberated feeling! I wanted to get up on my toes and run fast. And I did for a while. Toward the end of the hour, I felt a stinging sensation in my toes. When I finished the workout, I found my feet reddened by blood blisters, apparently the result of tiny bits of shell that were concealed underfoot. It hurt. Another two days off.

I regret that I did not commence serious running until 1972, because the previous summer we vacationed in the Southwest in many beautiful places. We drove the California coast from San Francisco to Los Angeles, and savored the Grand Canyon and other natural wonders while traveling through Nevada, Arizona, Colorado and New Mexico. I have to go back to the Grand Canyon, if for no other reason than to run there.

This is cross-country running. It is man meeting nature, not avoiding it. Much has been written lately about the emotional high attained from running long distances at a comfortable pace. It has been described as a euphoric state in which the rhythms of body and mind become compatible. This is true.

"Those possessing the stamina for close to an hour of steady running report an altered state of consciousness, a sudden rush of perceptive power coupled with an almost Zen-like peace." That's from a *Newsweek* cover story. This consciousness, this perception, this feeling of power is at its height on a cross-country run when the stimuli are most sensual and the feedback is most refreshing.

Get lost. Get away from the tracks and off the roads and run cross-country. Spurn the traffic and the noise and the polluted air. Say goodbye to the angry dogs and the jibing neighbors. Ignore time and distance and rigidity. Seek the fresh, the pure, the varied, the space. Feel the swoosh of your feet meeting the moist, pliable turf. Move from grass to gravel, from sand to leaves. Fool the wind by ducking amid the trees. Gallop the open spaces, up and down hills that you will favor, not fear, that will enrich your strength, not deflate it.

Take it all in. Absorb the sights and scents, and watch the seasons change with the foliage. The powers of observation grow: Little things will be noticed and pondered. Slight weather variances and terrain alterations will be detected. You will be finely tuned, and your senses

21

will be as radar, reacting to the most subtle stimuli. This is good, for when we are indifferent to our surroundings we do not help or protect them.

Turn me loose. Put me in New England in the fall, when the landscape catches fire with the changing colors of deciduous trees. The spectrum ranges from the delicate yellow of birch to the velvety purple of American ash, including almost every shade in between.

Put me in the Adirondacks where hardwood beeches, birches and maple grow from the High Peaks to the Lake Country. Put me in the foothills of the High Sierra where in April tiny wild flowers bloom before clusters of sycamores, oak and digger pines. Put me out in the canyons of Utah, on the hostile pathways of sunbaked rock and parched sand that meet the mountain mahogany. Put me in Bayou country, or shall I say near it, for I have not yet learned to run on water. Or put me in the Olympic forests of the Northwest where the tall evergreens diffuse the heavy rain. Or . . .

Regrettably, I usually settle for a lot less. Living in the concrete capital of the world, I try to make it to New York's wonderful parks. And they are wonderful. Each borough has several and one that is particularly contoured for running. There is Central Park in Manhattan. Add Prospect Park (Brooklyn, Van Cortlandt Park (Bronx), Forest Park (Queens) and Clove Lakes Park (Staten Island). Ted Corbitt, the legendary ultra-long distance runner and 1952 Olympic marathoner, once told me that he considered Prospect Park to be the finest place to train anywhere.

I also run on New York's golf courses and have yet to be chased by course officials. I skirt the perimeter, occasionally traversing a fairway and quickly dashing between clusters of trees. My footprints can also be found on parts of the Jamaica Bay Wildlife Refuge.

Recently, on an exploratory hunch, I discovered an excellent cross-country site only five miles from home. It's called High Rock Park, and I had been reading in the local paper, the *Staten Island Advance*, of nature walks conducted there. Where one can walk, one can usually run. So on a 100-degree summer day, I ventured there hoping at least to find a few miles of shade. What a treasure: several miles of fully-shaded, narrow trails, replete with cross-country obstacles like logs and bridges. A section of the park empties onto a golf course, making it possible to run an entire, varied workout without once hitting the public streets.

Although the autumn season with its moderate weather is the time when school leagues run cross-country, there is no calendar boundary, except what is imposed by precipitous weather in the remote regions of the country. Snow and rain and wind, when extreme, can make inviting land impassable.

Probably the factor that most threatens the sustained pleasures of running is its repetitiveness. I love lasagna, beer, sex, TV reruns of *The Honeymooners*, writing and playing with my daughter. But I don't duplicate these experiences without changing their frequency or content. So I must run around—all around—to spice the adventure with variety.

Run cross-country. Patronize the environment and it will thank you for it. While it can.

4
Its US Style

On Nov. 25, 1974, three days before Thanksgiving, two college runners from Ohio State and several others from Fordham University were miscast in a controversial role that symbolized one fragment of the current state of the sport of cross-country running in the United States. While the annual National College Athletic Association championship event was being run on a clear, cold morning in Bloomington, Ind., these men were protesting the denial of their right to compete by their respective universities.

More specifically, it was the athletic directors of these institutions who refused to permit the athletes to compete. They both claimed financial hardship (which I shall tell you about shortly). But if the A.D.'s are to be castigated, what about higher-ranking school officials, the trustees and even alumni who by their acquiescense provided tacit approval?

Fordham qualified its team for the NCAA by placing sixth out of 24 teams (third among District Two schools) in the IC4A meet in New York City. The school's A.D., Peter Carlesimo, told Coach Tom Byrne and his runners to stay home because they really weren't very good at cross-country.

"They just wouldn't have done well," he claimed. "They would have been outclassed. We're trying to build a Lombardi Center, and we're in tight times financially."

Lombardi, of course, is Vince Lombardi, the football legend and Fordham alumnus. His statement, "Winning isn't everything—it's the only thing," could have gotten him elected president—of anything.

Another apparent factor was that the Fordham swimming team spent a week at the Nationals in California the previous year and not one swimmer made it to the finals. At Fordham, if you don't win, you don't play in certain sports. It was estimated that it would have cost the team $1500 to make the Bloomington trip. Some of the runners offered to pay for the trip themselves. Carlesimo rejected that, too.

Coach Byrne said he was "disappointed" and added tactfully, "No one specifically told me the scholarships would be taken away, but you have to understand the school's feeling about image, especially at this time. We all want to build the (Lombardi) Center, and we don't want any bad reaction about our teams."

Fordham people aligned with Carlesimo's Lombardi mentality apparently did not take well to the runners' uprising nor to the sympathetic coverage it got in *The New York Times.*

Sportswriter Gerald Eskanasi wrote, "Fordham University's cross-country team staged its own 'national championships' in front of the athletic department in protest of the school's refusal to send the squad to the real national championships held yesterday." The story went on to explain that Fordham runners jogged in pairs around the portion of the campus known as Edwards Parade. It was to have lasted 24 hours.

"We're demonstrating for ourselves," said Gene McCarthy, one of the team members. "We've got to keep our morale up. No one seems to care that we earned the right to compete in the national championships."

Ohio State—the same Ohio State of *Goodbye Columbus* and Woody Hayes. Columbus is located about 200 miles east of Bloomington. It would have reduced A.D. Ed Weaver's multi-million dollar bankroll by a hundred bucks to send runners Tom Bryant and Tom Byers to the race. As in the Fordham case, Bryant's father called Weaver and offered to pick up the tab. Weaver refused.

At State, which sends football teams out to trample the country, they have this rule they dig out of the archives for special occasions. It requires a runner to place first or second in the Big Ten race in order to go to the NCAA meet. Bryant placed fifth; Byers was 30th. According to the complex NCAA qualifying system, both young men could run in Bloomington because of their respective ninth-and 20th-place finishes in the NCAA District Four meet, held one week after the Big Ten event.

Said Weaver, "We haven't deprived anybody of anything. I don't care about it."

Ohio State Cross-Country Coach Bob Epskamp preferred to "keep it an internal matter," no doubt for fear of reprisal, and accepted the decision.

Bryant said, "I was having my best season. I'm a senior and I had a legitimate shot at All-American (top 25 places). I've been running 100 miles a week since September."

Indiana Coach Sam Bell, the NCAA meet director, said, "I think it's a crime for any kid who qualified not to be allowed to run. The problem is the premise that unless it makes money, it's not worth doing."

Penn State Coach Harry Groves, president of the NCAA Cross-Country Coaches Association, said, "Most A.D.'s do not understand the total sports program. They base decisions on a single frame of reference—of how their kids rank nationally—which reflects a lack of understanding."

This tale is symptomatic of a greater ailment in this country. That is, the increasing preoccupation, attention and support given by the media and the public to professional and quasi-professional sports at the expense of athletic endeavors not tied to money—the so-called amateurs. That is why the average annual salary in the National Basketball Association can exceed $100,000 and Yankee Stadium can be refurbished at a cost of $100 million, while in communities across America scholastic sports budgets are slashed to the bone.

More relevant to the topic at hand, the Fordham/Ohio State posture—and don't think this sort of thing does not occur elsewhere—can surface because of the muddled place cross-country occupies within the present-day athletic stratum.

What's it for, anyway? Is it part of track and field? Does it serve track and field? Is it concerned with the road-running boom? With recent health crazes? Who does it? When? Why? How do we know who's best? Whaddaya mean it's a team sport? What about the Olympics?

There exists a devastating communications gap. People have heard of cross-country as a competitive sports fixture, but amid all the shades of running—and particularly the jogging roar—they don't know what to make of it. How then can we expect them to bitch when some kids are ordered to forget the Big Race and eat cake instead? If people are not directly involved in the sport, familiarity with it does not go beyond a short item about a local event in the evening paper or perhaps some confusion between cross-country running and cross-country skiing.

One of the reasons for the jogging and road running phenomenon is that all along people were aware of its scope. That scope, we have been drilled, has no boundary. Everyone can jog—anywhere, any time, any place and for any distance. And if you jog enough, you will be fit enough to run in races—which are held anywhere, any time, any place and at any distance. This is a wonderful sport, this free spirit of jogging, and we are delighted to find it worthwhile. Its ABC's are quite clear. We know what to do, what to buy, when to go and when to stop.

We also have the option to take the sport to its popular ultimate: the marathon. This 26-mile challenge is rooted in history, tradition and sacrifice, and conjures the romantic glow of runners on the plains of ancient Greece. We have seen the classic newsreels of the dazed Italian in baggy pants who collapsed near the finish of an Olympic Marathon, of the African who won with bare feet. We have seen the live telecasts of recent Olympic Marathons when boyish-looking Americans gained respect from their elder European opponents.

You start at Point A, proceed past B and C...and Z is your formula mile in under six minutes or your three-hour marathon. There is an appealing pattern to the sport of road running.

In addition to the positive factors of scope and destiny, road running has inherent spectator appeal. People are out there anyway, walking, shopping, socializing, doing business, mowing lawns. The race makes it all a happening, and good citizens line the streets for miles, if only to get a peek at the *Sports Illustrated* coverboy or the guy next door.

Cross-country has none of this mass market appeal, at least not in the US. It further suffers from its lack of standardization—which is ironic because that is, I think, part of its beauty. Distances and courses and rules vary, times mean little, the team element is unclear. Americans thrive on the convenience of standards. Businesses, like banks and sporting goods distributors, that sponsor road races prefer it this way. Baseball and other cultural sports symbols came from that mold. Track and field and the rest—they are precise.

So what is to be done? Must we compromise the natural appeal of cross-country in order to gain greater acceptance? No, but a few refinements and commitments may take things a long way:

1. *We have to open up cross-country.* It is almost exclusively a school-connected activity. It is an interscholastic and intercollegiate

sport conducted in the fall months, which means generally that if you're not between the ages of 15 and 22, it will be quite difficult for you to compete in cross-country in America. The something-for-everyone character of road running, with its 12-month cycle, proliferation of events and layered prize structure, is part of what makes it tick.

Road running administrators have an obligation here. So does the AAU. Their cross-country events, few and far between, represent tokenism. The New York Road Runner's Club and the local AAU there do a respectable job in this regard. Their 1977 schedule listed 10 cross-country races at Van Cortlandt Park, one in May, one in July and eight in the fall. Included were age-group, junior and Masters events. We need more of this, for when cross-country becomes accessible to the entire public, then the school leagues will prosper from the fallout of overall success.

2. *We have to distinguish cross-country from road running by capitalizing on cross-country's main attraction—the course.* Many cross-country routes are much too sterile and would even qualify as a road racing venue. Let us choose terrain that resembles what the Europeans use, with their chancy footing and natural obstacles. That will not turn away the applicants we wish to lure. Remember, road runners are constantly seeking new challenges, and don't they thrive on a 26-mile event? This admittedly is difficult since cross-country pathways are not at our front doors like the city streets.

3. *I would also like to see a pot at the end of the cross-country rainbow*—something that runners, all ages, men and women, could plan for and anticipate with zeal; something that functions for cross-country as the marathon does for general running.

Why not develop a standard 10-mile event, preferably a bit hilly, that would culminate a series of more "ordinary" cross-country races in given areas. Every branch of the Road Runner's Club or AAU could conduct one. Just call it Ten-Mile Cross-Country. Simple and direct. It would stick. It would have appeal. It would serve to further substantiate other cross-country events, which would lead up to the grand finale. No qualifying system, no restrictions. Find a large, wide-open site to attract a big field, plus viewers and the media. This could be the main element of a re-directed national cross-country program: Ten-Mile Cross-Country.

4. *Next, we have to take care of our champions.* We have to lead our *creme de la creme* on a productive path toward the International meet—not so much to elevate their chance to win as to fulfill our obli-

gations to field our best possible teams for this great worldwide event. Since this meet functions as the Olympics of cross-country, it must be given its proper respect.

Also, whenever credence is given to a kind of ultimate championship, the entire hierarchy of a sport accrues the benefits. The young runners will have something to dream about. The better-class runners will have something to aim for. We will know where we are headed. This is very important for cross-country.

US officials should continue to send to the International the maximum number of runners allowed to compete, but in the future even the last qualifiers—everyone—should have his or her trip entirely financed.

And why take this entourage of specialists to Europe for only one race? Set up a tour. Spend a week or more before and after the International running a few additional races in other countries. (In 1977, the US took a welcome step in this direction by going on to the famous Cinque Mulini cross-country race in Italy after the IAAF in Dusseldorf, West Germany.) This tour would be known as the annual International Cross-Country Tour. And what has greater appeal to the amateur athlete than a three-week competitive tour of Europe?

Our selection process for this arrangement should be altered a bit. For both the men's senior and women's teams, choose half of the qualifiers from the collegiate championships and the other half from the AAU's. Every possible contender has access to one or both of these events and at a time, in late fall, when they should be in peak condition. By December, the teams could be set up and the runners could go about their business for the ensuing indoor season before preparing for the March departure.

The junior (19 or under) men have no national event to use as a trial run. The two high school events that have national draw—the AAU Junior Olympics and AAU "Boys"—have an age ceiling and do not take in the 18- and 19-year olds who usually pace our squad. Thus, the current system of a separate junior trial is mandatory, but it should be held in December, not later, as a natural postscript to our fall season.

Speaking of our international teams, it wouldn't hurt the US to compete more with neighboring Canada. It wouldn't hurt Canada either. Skeptics may chide this need, for Americans meet large numbers of foreigners on home soil in the *US* college cross-country meets, a situation of considerable controversy to which I will address myself shortly.

So let's get on with it. Let us take this valuable sport of cross-country running and properly distinguish and define it, broaden its appeal, give it firm direction, putty up its loopholes, tighten its organization and encourage both the weak and strong among us to pursue it.

CROSS-COUNTRY AT THE OLYMPICS

I have not wasted time yelling at the Olympics for the absence of a cross-country race (although the renewal of Olympic cross-country would do wonders for the sport), since we have the annual International, and the International Olympic Committee does not hear yelling, anyway. At its most recent meeting, the ICC reinstated the 50-kilometer walk (which it had stupidly dropped from the 1976 Games) but refused to install any track event for women greater than the current topper of 1500 meters.

In 1912, 1920 and 1924, in Stockholm, Antwerp and Paris, there was cross-country in the Olympics. (The Berlin Games of 1916 were cancelled because of World War I.)

In 1912, Hannes Kolehmainen of Finland won the 8000-meter race after earlier acquiring the 5000 and 10,000 track titles. Sweden led the team scoring. Kolehmainen switched to the marathon in 1920 (and won), leaving the lengthened 10,000-meter cross-country race open to his countrymen Paavo Nurmi, possibly the greatest runner of the 20th century. Nurmi, the Flying Finn, triumphed and also captured the track 10,000. Then, there was Paris.

Within 90 minutes of the same afternoon, Nurmi won and set Olympic records in the 1500- and 5000-meter runs. Two days later, Nurmi successfully defended his 10,000-meter cross-country title. Jesse Abramson of the *New York Herald Tribune* later wrote:

"In sweltering heat that caused 24 of the 39 starters to faint, collapse or quit the grind in exhaustion, Paavo strode majestically over fields, pavements, fences and water jumps. Impervious to the heat and fatigue alike, he won effortlessly. The next day, with many of his cross-country opponents still hospitalized from their exertions, Nurmi was ready for another race. It wasn't an official part of the Olympic program, but he won the 3000-meter (cross-country) team race, leading his fellow Finns to victory."

Counting team awards, Nurmi collected six gold medals. They wouldn't let him also run the track 10,000. The cross-country event is among history's most memorable, not only for Nurmi's incomparable effort but for the debacle that caused it to be omitted from all succeeding Olympic programs to date.

As Abramson indicated, oppressive heat caused entrants to drop like

30

flies. It was July 12, and it was still a scorcher when the race went off at 4:30. Nurmi won by two minutes. He had not compromised his flawless style, even to the finish where he showed no signs of being upset by the conditions.

One runner entered the stadium gates in a daze, turned in the wrong direction and ran head-on into a concrete wall, splitting his scalp and falling to the ground covered with blood. Another runner suffered a heat stroke. Out in the country, men were lying scattered, some almost at death's door. Two and a half hours after the start of the race, unconscious runners were being found on the ill-fated route and given strychnine to save their lives.

As British writer F.A.M. Webster recalls it, "That was the most dramatic of the many hundreds of races that I have witnessed and when, finally, a game little Frenchmen struggled home with one foot bleeding and one shoe gone, the whole crowd rose to him and roared in acclamation."

THE HIGH SCHOOL SYSTEM

When I outlined some of the shortcomings of the US cross-country system, I hope I did not leave the impression that it is in total disrepair. It is quite alive and, if not in ideal health, then not in a state of calamity, either. Its foundation lies with the high schools and colleges.

High school cross-country exists as a regular team sport in all 50 states. All but a few states have girls' competition as well as boys'. Most school programs include a series of dual meets—one team against another team. These duals take up about two-thirds of the season. During this time, teams usually will venture into a small number of invitational runs with races containing as many as a few hundred runners from dozens of schools. Most schools also belong to leagues, which run championship meets for their members before the system of state-qualifying takes hold.

Commonly, one or two levels—called the district, sectional, regional or class meets—precede the "states." These meets are championships in themselves and also send the leading teams in the grand championships—the state finals. Thus, a runner might participate in about 10 races during the season.

Some states, like Ohio, hold the state meet at the same site every year. Others, like Vermont, rotate it. Some states, like West Virginia, hold one title race for all qualifiers. Others, like Iowa, hold races in several divisions based on school enrollment. In certain states, like Wisconsin, there are separate races or even entire meets for parochial or private schools. Ironically, every state except California, which is the undisputed leader in producing outstanding teenage distance running talent, conducts a statewide championship event. California goes no farther than sectional competition.

Mississippi was the last state to set up a championship meet. A 1976 report on the state of cross-country there said, "Many high schools fail to initiate a cross-country program because of the difficulty involved with securing a coach. Football claims the total attention of high school athletic departments in the fall. A majority of the coaches are involved within the football program. Most of the high school cross-country coaches are either football coaches who double up in the fall or faculty members who coach the team for little or no pay."

Most schools confine themselves to the progression of competition within their own state. Interstate events are on the rise, though, as ambitious coaches seek added stimuli for themselves and their runners. Geography is a big factor. Some teams can travel heavily without ever leaving their state's borders. The greatest pocket of interstate competition is in the Northeast, where the Eastern States and New England championship meets are among the more prestigious events. There is also some international activity among schools from our Northern border states (e.g., New York and Vermont) and Canada.

The state championships signal the end to the high school season. Top runners—individuals, not teams—have the option of going on to national scale competition. The AAU conducts separate boys and girls nationals plus a Junior Olympics meet that has boys' and girls' events on the same program. All three meets have rotating sites and have races set up according to age with 16-17 the oldest division. The aforementioned IAAF Junior Trials are also available to the high-caliber runner.

Invitational events, which can go on for hours, sometimes send off thousands of runners, broken up into fields of, say, 200 in repeated races over the same route. The races are designed to accommodate age or ability and are called varsity, junior varsity, freshmen, girls, etc. Prizes are plentiful.

High school teams run distances between two and three miles, with few exceptions. Because of the metric transitions, some three-mile events are turning into 5000 meters, or about 3.1 miles. Arizona has a few events that even exceed that, and its state meet distance is 3.3. Girls' races generally range between one and two miles, with a few states going beyond that.

As explained in greater detail elsewhere, scoring is done by adding

32

the places of the first five runners from a team to cross the finish line. A team that places its harriers 2-8-20-51-128 would score an aggregate of 209 points. Low score wins. The same is true for the colleges. An exception occurs in the high school ranks in rural Nebraska where in the small-schools division only four runners score.

In a typical state, the competitive season starts in mid-September and ends about eight weeks later, in early November. There are scattered meets at the very end of August in places where the school term commences shortly before that time. In Alaska, where winter comes early, cross-country ends early with a state meet at the beginning of October. Louisiana, Texas and California are the only states that take their seasons into December.

The recently published *Report of the President's Commission on Olympic Sports,* established by Gerald R. Ford in 1975, stated that 214,840 men and 12,301 women ran high school cross-country in 1974. (The women's figure is no doubt much larger now, with the application of Title IX regulations and the overall cultural changes influencing women's athletics.) We can break down the men's total further and estimate that the average high school team has perhaps 25-35 members. Some programs are truly remarkable, such as the one at Archbishop Molloy High in New York City where upwards of 150 harriers take part, depending on the size of the freshman class.

I have yet to come across a high school coach who held tryouts for his team, as is customary in most other sports where only a specified number of persons can play. All a youngster has to do to gain a position on a high school cross-country team is show up for practice. No matter how slowly he runs, he will not be cut from the squad. This is not to imply that little talent is required for cross-country. Yes, only moderate skills may get one a team jacket, but a package of abundant talent is essential for *success.* And that is the way it should be: Let every willing youngster run, but single out the gifted and the dedicated.

There exists a State High School Athletic Association for each state, governing the activity of all scholastic sports. Virtually all schools are members; otherwise, they could not participate in the state championships and gain a host of other services such as inexpensive insurance coverage. On the minus side, it also means that member schools must abide by its rules which at times are restrictive. For example, a team may be forbidden from competing in more than two meets per week, from having organized practice in the presence of a coach prior to September 1, or from running in an "open" AAU-type race during the regular season.

These State Associations, in turn, comprise the National Federation of State High School Athletic Associations, with offices located in the Chicago suburb of Elgin, Ill. The Federation was established in 1920 and has a membership of all 50 states and nine affiliated Canadian provinces. The states function as agencies of the National Federation, enforcing its rules and carrying out its policies. It sees itself as Big Daddy. From its handbook:

"The National Federation was organized primarily to secure proper adherence to the eligibility rules of the various state associations in interstate contests and meets. The activities (of the N.F.) are based on the belief that strong state and national high school athletic organizations are necessary to protect the activity and athletic interests of the high schools, to promote an ever increasing growth of a type of interscholastic athletics which is educational in both objective and method, and which can be justified as an integral part of the high school curriculum to protect high school students from exploitation for purposes having no educational implication."

Coach Elton Wright of Jackson, Miss., has used on the national level some of the same energies that have advanced cross-country in his state. Wright is chairman of the cross-country committee of the National High School Athletic Coaches Association. This committee is doing fine work in its intended areas of gathering and disseminating information, acquiring historical perspective, promoting and publicizing cross-country and making rules recommendations to the National Federation.

The group was organized in 1975. It has awarded Coach-Of-The-Year plaques to John C. Coughlan, Maine East High School, Park Ridge, Ill.; Brent Haley, Largo High School, Largo, Fla.; and Joe Newton, York High School, Elmhurst, Ill.

Newton, a dynamic figure, is probably the best-known high school track and cross-country coach in the United States. Besides developing consistently successful teams in a highly competitive state in his 20 years on the job, Newton is accomplished as a meet director, lecturer and writer. He has helped put cross-country on the map in Illinois. Twice, several busloads of York students plus a pep band made the 300-mile round-trip to the state finals and greeted the triumphant Dukes with a wild reception.

Newton is a stickler for discipline and dedication. In 1969, he co-authored *The Long Green Line*. An excerpt: "Our runners must go through hurt, pain and agony. They have to keep going when the body is crying out to quit. There is no tranquilizer in sports....At York, they

34

run not for their life but for their honor. They run for tradition. At York, they run because when they run, it has meaning!"

There are many other extraordinary high school programs throughout the country. Among the most conspicuous, in terms of consistent success, are those at South Eugene High School, Eugene, Ore., Central High School, Cheyenne, Wyo.; Handley High School, Winchester, Va.; Largo High School, Largo, Fla.; and St. Joseph's, Buffalo, N.Y.

THE U.S. COLLEGES

The talented high school runners in the US move along a predictable path. They are recruited by colleges that seek to be competitive in both cross-country and track. The exceptional runners receive many offers for full athletic scholarships, valued in many cases at $20,000 or more for a four-year education.

There is no need here to analyze the cumbersome financial aid regulations except to point out that, although abuse of these rules does not begin to approach that of the big-time college sports of football and basketball, it does exist in cross-country. Relative to scholarships, two controversial issues have risen in the 1970s. One has tended to unify the cross-country community, and the other has divided it.

The unifying factor has been something bad. Harmful things tend to unify the downtrodden. In January 1976, the NCAA voted to reduce the number of track scholarships to be granted over any given four-year period from 23 to 14. "Track" includes cross-country, and there is nothing additional for cross-country. That limitation represented a 39% reduction. Football was cut from 120 to 90, a 25% reduction; basketball from 18 to 15, a 16-2/3% loss.

This situation has unified cross-country people in their attempt to legislate against it. But it has also made colleges more competitive—put them at greater odds with each other—in trying to land prominent scholastic athletes.

In October 1975, in anticipation of the new rulings, *The Harrier* magazine editorialized:

"How many young kids will be turned off from track and cross-country because they know that no matter what they do, short of real star status, the opportunities awaiting them will be few and far between? And how many Olympic and national stars were once so-so kids who got a break, showed extraordinary talent, found a good coach and worked their tails off all the way to the top? Now, you'll find many of these guys getting into trouble rather than getting into a track suit."

The other issue is more complicated and more volatile. It concerns

35

the tendency of many colleges to recruit athletes from other countries to boost their teams, instead of recruiting American schoolboys. This issue becomes most inflamed at the time of the national championships, since foreigners usually come away with many of the top honors.

Years ago, when this started to occur, these foreigners were typically from Canada, Great Britain, Ireland, Scandinavia and the Caribbean. They still come from those places, but now the majority of incoming athletes come from African nations, of which Kenya is the leader. These students frequently enter US schools at age 21 or older, which distinguishes their athletic capacities and experiences from those of 18-year-old college freshmen.

At the 1976 NCAA Championships in Denton, Texas, foreign athletes from the University of Texas at El Paso, Washington State and other schools, from dozens of towns across Europe and Africa, captured seven of the first 10 places and 17 of the top 50. UTEP's team was first and Washington State, led by the victorious Kenyan Henry Rono, finished third.

The previous year, in University Park, Pa., UTEP also triumphed— by four points over Washington State. Eight of the 10 scoring runners from these teams were foreigners. Seven of the eight were Kenyans. Providence, with four Irishmen, placed third. Harry Groves, the meet director and coach of fourth-place Penn State, was heard to say, "We won the *American* championship."

Inevitably, two philosophical camps have formed. Those with foreign athletes and their sympathizers represent one viewpoint. Those without the foreigners—either because of conviction or lack of connections— are the opponents. There are valid points made by both sides.

The proponents claim that the presence of foreigners enhances competition, stimulates American athletes, stabilizes teams (because of the foreign athletes' appreciative attitudes), reveals novel training techniques, balances recruiting power and adds an attractive cultural diversity to a team and school.

Opponents maintain that the foreigners inhibit American runners, take scholarships away from US preps, create unfair competition, use *our* facilities as an Olympic training ground and further subvert the recruiting system, because they are marginal students at best.

Taking the entire matter into consideration myself, I am of the opinion that foreign athletes should be permitted to compete on US teams in cross-country (and other sports), but that there should be a ceiling placed on their number and age. However, age is difficult to verify, since African birth records are not easily documented. (To backtrack a bit, on Dec. 10, 1973, US District Court Judge Gerhard Gesell struck down an NCAA age-eligibility rule for "aliens" and, in effect, enabled college coaches to recruit foreign athletes without regard to age.)

Although I am firm in this belief, I am not comfortable with it, for it is disturbingly regressive in certain ways. Perhaps more time must pass so that the effects of the phenomenon can become clearer, and judgments can be made more wisely and less emotionally.

Foreigners coming to the US find a well-motivated college cross-country system for men and women that is based on a primary goal of conference and national honors. They run several dual meets and perhaps one or two invitationals before conference, district and national events.

All of the major conferences, such as the Big Ten, Southeast and Pacific-Eight, have cross-country championships. So do the more obscure leagues such as the Great Plains, Heart of America and Gulf South. From there, teams go on to district meets, which serve as qualifying for the nationals.

The most prominent cross-country meet in the United States is the NCAA Division I (large schools) Championship. Teams qualify for this meet through regional meets. District qualifying also exists for the National Association of Intercollegiate Athletics (NAIA) and National Junior College Athletic Association (JUCO) events but not for the NCAA Division II and III (small-schools) chapters. Where district qualifying applies, full teams advance, as do high-placing individuals who are not members of qualifying teams. Where it does not exist, only full teams can participate, and membership in the association is the only criterion for entry. The exception is the AAU championship, open to both unattached and club/team-affiliated runners who are AAU members.

Another national organization is the United States Track and Field Federation (USTFF), born out of the political struggles between the NCAA and AAU. This "open" federation conducts what it calls a national meet but secures only a meager and unpredictable entry.

College men at four-year schools usually compete at distances of either five or six miles or their rough metric equivalents of 8000 or 10,000 meters. The junior colleges recently moved from four to five miles for their national meet but have expressed a reluctance to go up to 10,000 meters—which, I think, will soon become the accepted American collegiate cross-country distance. College women run between two and three miles, or 5000 meters.

RACE COURSES

The sites used on both the scholastic and collegiate levels are mainly what is available, and they will safely accommodate the number of anticipated runners. Colleges rely on campus grounds and golf courses and, to a lesser degree, on public parks. High schools first turn to parks, and secondarily frequent school grounds and golf courses.

Imagine the reactions of golf course engineers if they knew their best-laid plans for nine-irons were to receive wider application. Even though practical and legal concerns—and even the desire for fast performances—preclude ingenuity in establishing course design, there exist a great many charming cross-country routes. They are appealing either for their simple beauty or their uniqueness.

In Hawaii, where four of the islands have cross-country competition, some races are run right through the sand and surf of the famous beaches. Rural roads, city roads, forests and farmland are also used, along with the grounds of a hospital and cemetery. "We run meets any place we can," reports one coach.

Another of these charmers is Fountainhead Regional Park in Lorton, Va., home course for George Mason University in nearby Fairfax. It is a five-mile route. G.M. assistant coach Norm Gordon describes it:

"The course begins on a macadam road, and in the first mile includes three gradual 100-yard hills and one hairpin turn. Miles two, three and four are on two nature trails with a maximum width of 10 feet. In those three miles, a runner will make 51 turns of 45-degree angle or greater (18 of them greater than 90 degrees), climb five sets of 'natural' steps, descend two sets of steps, climb and descend six steep hills of between 30 and 50 yards, cross seven narrow bridges and run through three streams.

"The last mile is relatively easy. It includes a 200-yard downhill slope and culminates with a 300-yard steep incline in the last quarter-mile. It is a difficult course to run due to the constant turning, the blind corners and the hills. It has been described by an opposing coach as 'fit only for billy goats.'"

This is an ambitious course, just as cross-country is an ambitious sport. This drive is perhaps more evident in the size and scope of some meets, which have admirably sought to open their trails and their hearts to a wide cross-section of the running community.

There is the 73-year-old Dipsea, the quintessential cross-country race, that snakes about seven miles over and through the hills between Mill Valley and Stinson Beach, Calif. This race melds almost every possible running challenge into a one-shot free-for-all. For the card-carrying adventurers, there is also the Double Dipsea, which requires running from Stinson Beach to Mill Valley *and back.*

Another special California roast is the Mount San Antonio College meet, a sort of cross-country Penn Relays in that the entire spectrum of runners takes part: colleges, high school, junior high, little kids and masters, men and women, open and novice. It adds up to more than 6000 athletes in scores of races spread over three days. The races on the campus offer enough prizes to stock a department store at Christmas time.

Prizes are also in abundance at the Manhattan College affair in New York City, the second largest meet in the country. More than 5000 runners, girls and boys representing 250 schools from nine states, raced in a series of 21 divisions on the Van Cortlandt Park trails in the 1976 edition. Unfortunately, the meet has been plagued with rain since its inception in 1973, prompting sideliners to joke that Manhattan College should put a dome over the park and conduct the world's first indoor cross-country meet.

5
Its Teamwork

In baseball, a home run slugger can lead a team to the World Series. In football, a fleet and nimble running back can take a team to the Super Bowl. In basketball, a towering center can bring a team to the championship. And in soccer and hockey and most other team sports, a team can have flaws, failures and misfortunes but still succeed because of the superstar, the athlete who does it all when it has to be done. Errors, missed shots, dropped passes, an unguarded net—they can be overcome by the likes of Johnny Bench, Julius Erving, O. J. Simpson, Pele or other heroes of recent years.

Cross-country is different. It is a team sport in the purest sense of the word. Cross-country squads do have superstars and have won honors because of them. But this can happen only when the supporting cast of runners achieves success in its own right. Many a team, even with four superior harriers, has finished a race out of the money because the key fifth man "got lost" in the hills. At a post-season banquet, when the sting of defeat has been soothed by the passage of time, the athletes may joke of the guy "who's still running."

In considering cross-country as a group endeavor, a curious ambivalence is suggested. The nature of the scoring is what requires a collective effort; yet, the runners perform, it seems, unilaterally. Each one runs as fast as he can over a specified route of a given distance, perhaps without giving the slightest thought of a teammate. He may think only of himself. He may think of the opposition in order to improve his time or boost his competitive zeal. He is not waiting for a pass or a throw or a block or a baton as his counterparts are in other sports. Cross-country runners handle their assignments independently, not interdependently—so they think. Where, then, is the team concept applied, other than in the cold numbers of post-race scoring?

Unfortunately, not in many places, for too many coaches omit from their programs the theory and practice of team running. This is probably because most cross-country coaches also head the track team, cross-country's cousin. Track and field, with its varied events and diverse training methods, *is* basically an individual sport, even when teams compete against one another. Triple jumpers have little in common with, say, milers, and coaching philosophy is understandably different in this area.

In cross-country, though, there is one event—The Race. Frequently, the track coach, upon moving into the cross-country season, continues to think and act in terms of individual progress, unaware of the values of a team-oriented approach. However, there are refreshing exceptions.

DEVELOPING TEAM FEELINGS

Larry Heidebrecht, cross-country coach at New Mexico Junior College, formerly headed the teams at Central High School in Cheyenne, Wyo. Every summer, about mid-August, Heidebrecht would round up his team, gather some camping gear together and head off to Encampment, Wyo., to train at 9000-foot altitude. This would last for a week or so, depending upon the amount of money the runners had been able to save. The team gained much more than the physical benefits of altitude training.

"We lived together and learned to respect one another," said Heidebrecht. "That is an important factor in cross-country running." The Central squad is annually one of the outstanding prep teams in the Rockies and has won many Wyoming state championships.

In the summer of 1972, a group of distance men from Lompoc High School in Southern California would get together twice a day for some casual running and conversation. They ran an occasional road race. A couple of the runners were more talented than the others, but they still ran with the others, poking fun and doing what comes naturally when

41

teenage boys sweat through a pleasant 10-mile workout.

When the important fall cross-country meets arrived, they were ready. As a group, Lompoc ran unbeaten during the regular campaign and then established a national high school record of 46:20.9 for the five-man, 10-mile relay.

"We worked together so well," recalls Steve Galbraith, who went on to college running. "That's why we were the best. We had a fantastic team spirit. We were known as the Magnificent Seven, a nickname given to us by teams in the Los Angeles and San Diego areas. We would line up for a race, and other teams would stare at us. It gave me an eerie feeling."

At Western High School in Las Vegas, Coach Dean Weible does not conform to the tempo of the town; he does not gamble. In the summers, "we have organizational meetings, go swimming, have barbeques and log our miles together." In the fall, Weible compiles a "Goal Pace Chart" that catalogs the development of each runner from the slowest to the fastest man on the team. Western has twice been crowned Nevada state champion and is virtually unbeaten in dual-meet competition over a six-year period.

Out in the deeper recesses of New York's Long Island, the Port Jefferson runners work out together all summer, attend a running camp prior to the cross-country season and train at 6 a.m. before classes in September. Coach Jim Smith wouldn't have it any other way.

"By the time our first meet comes along," says Smith, "each youngster is sensitive to the needs and capacities of his teammates." The Royals were the number-two rated team in the state in 1976 and won the state title for medium-sized schools.

Sam Bair, who ran a sub-four-minute mile while at Kent State University, coaches cross-country at Allegheny Community College in Pittsburgh. Bair inherited the team from Neil I. Cohen, who retains an advisory role now that he is the Allegheny athletic director. Both men employ the same philosophy.

"Every runner who makes our team," says Bair, "has a role in the scoring and a responsibility to his teammates. Each of them gets points, and those points are extremely important all the way down the line. Cross-country offers the best of both worlds. A runner gets to run his own race, but at the same time he gets to sample the good vibrations that come with team effort and unity. . . . We encourage our runners to stay in a group as long as is possible and practical. The strong ones thereby pull the weaker ones along. We try to use team strategy whenever we run."

Allegheny won the National Junior College championship in 1976 with the lowest point total in the meet's history. Since 1968, it has not lost in more than a hundred dual meets against junior college opposition.

Eugene, Ore., has been called the "Running Capital of the United States." And for good reason. There, the masses consider running a desirable way of life, not an aberration or a fashionable diversion from other sports. The University of Oregon's track and cross-country teams have acquired a national reputation, and its Hayward Field facility has hosted a number of championship events. Not far from the university is South Eugene High School, where cross-country Coach Harry Johnson relates the posture and temperance of his star harrier of the mid-1970s, Bill McChesney.

When some of the South runners were knuckling under to an especially grueling workout, such as repeated sprints up a steep sand dune, McChesney would pull up beside them and urge them on. "He'd get them to run faster than they ever thought possible," says Johnson. "He didn't have to do that, but he cared about them."

South Eugene won the Oregon State title in 1976 and was rated the number-two high school team in the country. The unbeaten McChesney was honored as the nation's outstanding individual runner.

"We try to use team strategy," states Coach Marshall Clark of Stanford University. "Obviously, it doesn't always work. The strength and ability of our runners in comparison with the competition is a big factor." Clark has coached many outstanding distance runners, including US Olympians Don Kardong and Duncan Macdonald.

Bill Silverberg of New Mexico University says, "We try to run together as long as they can, and then its everyone for himself near the end of the race. I really believe this helps the slower boy who might otherwise drop off and let the others go on. . . . It's a team effort, and all seven boys have to work together."

Before moving to New Mexico U., Silverberg coached at Eastern New Mexico, and his teams won the NAIA national titles in 1973 and 1974. His top runner was Mike Boit, a Kenyan, who captured the 1974 and 1975 NAIA events and is recognized as a world-class half-miler.

These coaches and their teams must be doing something right. Whether it's barbeques, camping out, training at daybreak or pack running, the patterns are consistent. Consider cross-country as a team sport in all phases of a program, and the experience will be a more fulfilling one for all those involved. You might even win something big.

It is important to point out parenthetically that the valuable personal approach a coach can cultivate with his athletes prior to the season would represent a violation of high school rules in some states. Some rulebooks are quite dogmatic in prohibiting a coach from meeting with his athletes prior to a specified date, which usually coincides with the beginning of the fall semester. But this is not to say that these restrictions are not regularly bent or compromised, in light of the difficulty in enforcing them.

SPLIT DECISIONS

There is no formula that will automatically mold a team of cross-country runners into a cohesive unit of unselfish participants, each out to help one another as he would help himself. Before examining ways to make a team out of individuals, it is important to know what the ideal is.

Experienced coaches refer to something called the "split" or "spread." No, not the split of relay runners; this is different. The split is the amount of time between the finish of a team's first runner and last runner in a given race. Since a maximum of seven runners usually can compete in one race, the split refers to the difference in finish time between a team's number-one and number-seven runner. Often coaches also compute the split for the scoring runners, and since only five runners score, that split will be less than the one for the entire unit.

The analysis of team splits is an essential tool in cross-country. Generally, the longer the distance of a race, the wider the split tends to be. Runners may be closely bunched over two miles but considerably spread out over three miles as distinctions in talent become more apparent. The same pattern is common when going from a flat course to one that may contain hills and rough terrain, and makes more demands on the athletes. The job of tightening a split becomes most difficult when faced with a rugged 10,000-meter layout, the longest distance used by American college teams. (Incidentally, the presence of an outstanding runner may distort the numerical value of a split, and a wise coach would then base his split on all runners except his champion.)

Let us take a look at the splits attained by the 1976 national collegiate team champions:

44

Meet	Winner	Distance	Victory Margin	Split*	
NCAA-I	Texas-El Paso	10 kilos	55 points	49	seconds
NCAA-II	Cal-Irvine	10 kilos	23 points	75	seconds
NCAA-III	North Central	8 kilos	23 points	48	seconds
NAIA	Edinboro State	5 miles	47 points	54	seconds
Jr. College	Allegheny	5 miles	100 points	29	seconds
AIAW	Iowa State	3 miles	48 points	56	seconds

*split is for five scoring runners

The average split for the six titlists is 52 seconds for their five scoring runners. If we assume that these runners were averaging a pace of about five minutes per mile, a 52-second split means that, theoretically, the first runner beat the fifth runner to the finish by about 300 yards. (Since most runners "kick in" at the end of a race, the margin may actually be theorized as a bit more than 300 yards.)

It is interesting to note that 300 yards represents only 3.6% of the entire race distance of 10,000 meters. This split, or gap, is perhaps not as difficult to trim as we have come to think. Moreover, a couple of the above teams had a runner who won or came close to winning the individual title, separating himself quite a bit from the rest of the team. Other teams, such as California-Irvine, bunched three or four runners very tightly up front but had a lagging "backfield" (fourth and fifth scorers).

In each case, the team concept is highly visible. The average winning point total was 58 and the average margin of triumph was 49 points. A weak link in any of those squads might have resulted in defeat, not victory.

Further evidence of successful team balance is found on the high school level. Here are the nation's five top-rated high school teams for 1976, from the pages of *The Harrier* magazine. Their state championship victories are charted below.

1976 TOP FIVE HIGH SCHOOL TEAMS

Team	Distance	Victory Margin	Points	Split*	
1. Deerfield (Ill.)	3 miles	31 points	111	29	seconds
2. South Eugene (Ore.)	5 kilos	65 points	62	74	seconds
3. Handley (Va.)	3 miles	39 points	30	56	seconds
4. Costa Mesa (Cal.)	2 miles	75 points	39	26	seconds
5. Bay Village (Ohio)	2 miles	39 points	102	21	seconds

*split is for five scoring runners

The average five-man split is 41 seconds, or about 235 yards based on five-minute mile pace. The teams with the widest splits are those with individual winners—Handley (Scott Haack) and South Eugene (Bill McChesney). We see a pattern here that at first glance may seem paradoxical. Deerfield and Bay Village and had very tight splits—but also had the smallest margins of victory and the highest (meaning the least desirable) winning point totals. However, the competition was keener in the Illinois—and Ohio races than in the other three events.

What happens when there exists the imbalance of a weak fifth runner placing well behind the front four? In the 1976 NCAA meet, Boise State, the Big Sky Conference champion, was justified in expecting a finish in the top 10 of 34 participating teams. But Boise's fifth scorer finished in 249th position, about a minute and a half behind his nearest teammate. Had this runner been able to run closer to this teammate, Boise would have scored perhaps 70 fewer points and placed 12th, a few points out of its goal of 10th.

TEAM SPIRIT

Some runners simply are able to run much faster than others. However, there are methods at the disposal of a coach that will enable him or her to develop a team-oriented sensitivity in runners, thereby tightening the split, reducing the score and elevating the team's and coach's success.

It is incumbent upon a coach to educate athletes about the team dynamics of cross-country. Most likely, runners are inclined to consider their efforts along individual lines, either because of their grooming in track and field or their natural competitive instincts.

They must be taught a kind of new math—the numbers of cross-country with its unusual scoring systems and subtleties. They must be taught that in many cases the stopwatch is of little value, and there are intangible ingredients that must be brewed for cross-country success. They must sincerely believe they are part of a group effort, despite the occasional instances of intrasquad competition. While other chapters are devoted entirely to such matters as organization, training and racing, let us examine those elements briefly as they relate to team strategy.

A team should be divided into groups of perhaps 7-10 runners, based preferably on ability, or on class in school or age. Each group should train apart from the others with varied intensity, depending upon the capacity of the runners.

The speed and distance of the workouts should be within the range of the weakest member of the group. There should be a gradual increase in the difficulty of the training, so as to develop mental and physical conditioning simultaneously. Every runner in a unit should be made to feel comfortable with his teammates and confident that he can run with them.

The youngsters should be encouraged to mingle on and off the course, and to develop pride in the training progress of the group. The very best runners should not be stifled; they can be given latitude without becoming detached from the others, such as with additional running after a regularly scheduled workout has been completed.

This policy should be extended, as much as possible and practical, into actual races. Goals should be based on running as a unit, not on time specifications. The coaching thrust should be: "If you'll stay together, you'll win (or at least do well)." Under meet conditions, the top runner (who may also be the team's captain) shoulders a lot of responsibility. The specific tactics in a race are based on numerous factors relating to the size of the race, opposition, weather, terrain, etc.

Let us take a hypothetical racing situation and apply team dynamics to it. First, the dual meet. Based on five-man totals, the closest a score can be (without tying) is 27-28. This would happen if, for example, Team A placed its seven runners 1-3-5-8-10 (27)-11-12 and Team B finished 2-4-6-7-9 (28)-13-14. The runners are fairly well spread out, but if any of the three slowest runners from Team B had been able to run with its number-four man, Team B might have won. "If..." examples can be illustrated ad infinitum. Yet the premise is still true regarding tight team running.

Sometimes, knowledgeable coaches ask a runner to "key" not only on a teammate but also on a particular opposing runner who is believed to be of the same ability. In dual meets with small fields, there is more of that type of man-to-man matchups.

Then, there is the medium-sized race that may have five or 10 schools with fewer than 100 runners scheduled to compete. In this type of event, there is the greatest opportunity for team unity to work. If an attempt is made to stay bunched for part of the race, the top runners will still have room to make their all-out bids because the route will not be too congested.

In a large invitational or championship event, the exceptional harrier must seek good position, but the rest of the unit can work together. Remember, the main reason for group running is to avoid having a letdown by a fourth or fifth scorer. If a gold medal contender must, at times, settle for second or even eighth, to help his team win, so be it.

This is tantamount to situations in basketball in which an outstanding shooter must pass the ball, lowering his point output but helping the overall team effort.

Make no mistake about it—running in a group does improve performance. When running apart from one's friends and teammates, it is easy to yield to the physical stresses of the moment. When rubbing shoulders with a set of familiar and trusted colleagues, it is easier to ignore the discomforts of a hard pace and push through the barrier that one may have unconsciously established for oneself.

It takes time to develop the team concept in cross-country running. The beauty of it is that it will make the hard work seem more like fun, and even if the desired gratification takes longer than expected, the experience of running as a team will leave an indelible impression upon one's athletic life.

Part Two:
RACES

6
Van Cortlandt: Mecca

Cross-country. Time trial. 21:10. I stopped five times. Terrible experience. First time on course.

I wrote that in September 1962 in my 3 x 5-inch diary of running experiences at Sheepshead Bay High School in Brooklyn. It was my junior year, and I was not quite 16 years old. That was my first "race" and thus my first diary entry. I was initiated at Van Cortlandt Park.

My only other notes for the run were: *Other times: Rosa and Davis, 16:50; Ingo, 18:03; Schwartz and Herpsman, 21:00. Four Horsemen— 15:10-15:40.*

Ingo was Eddie Ingerman, who the next year became our cross-country captain and broke the school record by 21 seconds with a time of 14:11 for the 2.5-mile circuit. The performance was good enough to place him 11th in the Brooklyn borough championships, a meet with 20-plus schools and a field with the disposition of TV's "Sweathogs."

Ingo, on the other hand, was very modest and unassuming. Dark-complexioned with close-cut black hair and heavy eyebrows, Eddie ran with an odd gait, taking choppy steps and moving his arms and torso from side to side. He trained very hard and sometimes ran more than five miles at once at a brisk pace. He even ran on Sundays, when the rest of us were playing football. Of this, we were in awe. We called him "The Animal."

The Four Horsemen were Roger Weiss, Howie Korn, George Pappas and Joel Goldberg. We called Pappas "Goose" because of his long neck. ("Nice and loose like a long-necked goose," we chanted in practice.) This quartet was a year ahead of my close friends and me, and was a stabilizing factor in tipping us off to the subleties of anticipated circumstances. They would give us advice as though they were older college fraternity brothers. This advice was particularly valuable during the indoor track season when we competed at "The Armory," from which we were lucky to escape with our limbs and our wallets.

Weiss went to college in Buffalo where, I believe, he studied dentistry. Korn went to Kent State in Ohio. Pappas went down to some place in South Carolina and was rumored to have left before the end of two years. I met Goldberg many years later while I served on jury duty in State Supreme Court in Brooklyn. He was an assistant district attorney. I was working on a murder case.

They were a great bunch of guys and took advantage of any opportunity to have fun. There were marathons—snowball fights, not footraces—and post-practice football games (after the coach had left). They harmonized the pop tunes of the day and organized sprint relay challenges between distance runners and shot putters. The shot putters always won.

These kids enjoyed themselves too much to win anything, although our team placed seventh in the 90-team public schools championships without the benefit of Goldberg. He missed the end of the season after cutting his foot on a piece of glass.

Our coach was Dick Lerer, a fine man who made up for his lack of training knowledge—who knew much in those days?—with the proper balance of drive and sensitivity. He later earned his doctoral degree and is now a top-ranking school administrator in a suburban district north of New York City.

At Van Cortlandt, Lerer would cry to me during a race, usually when I looked shell-shocked, "C'mon Bloom—blossom!" It didn't work. I wilted. My best time was only 17:42, a pace I would run years later for an entire 26-mile marathon. My diary comment of that 17:42: *Felt good except for pain in side. Could have ran (sic) under 17:00 if it wasn't for pain.* Sure.

I was one of the team's weakest cross-country runners, even in my senior year. This embarrassed me only a little because, after all, quarter-milers were not supposed to be fast at the longer distances. We were above that. Sprinters were *de riguer* then; pure cross-country men were a little crazy, and they had no real talent. Not like us: we ran cross-country to get in shape for indoors, when we would turn a few tricks at The Armory.

I often ran in the scrub division. Now *that* embarrassed me. In the larger meets, there were varsity, junior varsity and scrub races. Could there have been a more pejorative label? I think that contributed to my poor showing. I became a scrub. I could also point to the moderate training we did, but in retrospect I think my main shortcoming was that I could not cope with the discomfort, the pain of racing 2.5 miles of hilly Van Cortlandt terrain. I did not have the wherewithal to run "through" the numbness, the side stitches, the tumbling stomach. It hurt, and I could not subdue it.

Kids from suburban schools with long names came to Van Cortlandt on chartered buses, out of which they filed with fancy sweatsuits and a few gorgeous girl-managers with stopwatches resting in their cleavage. (Nowadays, girls have their own teams, too.) Their uniforms had printed on them the team nickname—Lions, Bruins, Wildcats, Patriots—for Most Holy Catholic Regional or Northeast Mohawk Valley does not fit on one jersey.

We took the subway. Sheepshead Bay is near Coney Island, the southern tip of New York City, not counting Staten Island, which most people don't. Van Cortlandt Park lies in the North Bronx and touches affluent Westchester County. It was a 40-mile, one-hour trip by car. It took us two hours. Walk to the bus, bus to the subway, subway to 42nd Street, crossroads of the world, for the Uptown Local, all the way up, past The Armory and Harlem to Broadway and 242nd Street. End of the line.

For us, the trip home was a festival, if a weary one. The race was behind us. Forget about medals. Our reward was a hero sandwich and a quart container of orange juice from one of the two nearby delicatessans, which are as much a part of the Van Cortlandt experience, even today, as anything. The Broadway Deli is the one right near the subway entrance. The shop, long and narrow, is a haven for those bent on pocketing an apple on the way out. That is why a clerk is always stationed at the door on autumn Saturdays.

What a group of seniors. Lane Schwartz, Joel Karasik, Richie Prager, Bob Davis, Mike Zebersky, Howie Sachs, Robert Weintraub, Fred Nekrich among them. We could have had our own Maccabiah Games team. Nekrich and I became infatuated with the statistical end of the sport, especially during the track seasons. We organized betting pools that peeved Coach Lerer to no end, for teammates became more interested in the morning line than in their own performances. Fred and I sat next to each other in a physics class and talked about a promising runner named Jim Ryun. That's why I failed physics the first semester. We had wet dreams about the event listings in *Track & Field News.*

Then, the roof fell in. Suddenly, Fred Nekrich died. It was early spring, in '64. We knew Freddie was bedridden with a bad cold. One morning, I got a call from Lane Schwartz, the eternal joker. This time he was solemn. "I've got bad news. . . ." I cried, and tears still well up in my eyes when I think about it. The entire team paid a condolence call to the Nekrich family one evening. The school started an annual sports award in Fred's memory.

Van Cortlandt Park is America's cross-country mecca. It is not paradise by any means. It has not the prettiest course nor the most difficult. It does not have the best facilities. It is just that it lies smack in the middle of the most populous megalopolis, in an area rich in cross-country tradition, where sponsors and those of influence have chosen to operate. Located as it is on the fringe of New York City, Van Cortlandt is most accessible. Public transportation funnels there from every neighborhood in the city. The subways are close by. Highways and turnpikes reach from the park to the distant locales of neighboring states.

Therefore, in a given season, more runners race its trails than any other cross-country site in the nation, if not the world. There are several distinct programs that merge at "Vanny," as it is sometimes called. The biggest is for the high schools. Iona College, Manhattan (and before it NYU), St. John's and Fordham sponsor meets with a combined entry in excess of 10,000.

The Manhattan meet is the nation's second largest cross-country meet. The Fordham meet has a special division that functions as the Eastern States Championships. There are many other league and city championship contests, starting in mid-September and ending in late November, that add several thousand to that figure. The New York State Championships alternate between Van Cortlandt and a suburban or upstate site.

There must be a hundred college dual meets at the park. Some of them involve schools from Boston and Washington and Philadelphia which use Van Cortlandt as a neutral site in terms of terrain and travel.

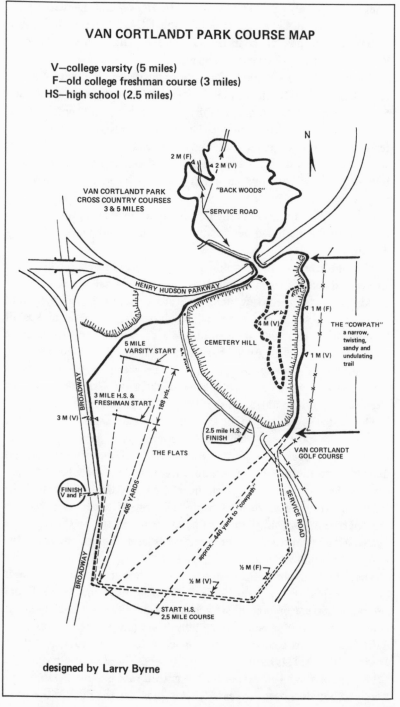

VAN CORTLANDT PARK COURSE MAP

V—college varsity (5 miles)
F—old college freshman course (3 miles)
HS—high school (2.5 miles)

2 M (F)

2 M (V)

N

VAN CORTLANDT PARK
CROSS COUNTRY COURSES
3 & 5 MILES

"BACK WOODS"

SERVICE ROAD

HENRY HUDSON PARKWAY

1 M (F)

4 M (V)

THE "COWPATH"
a narrow,
twisting,
sandy and
undulating
trail

5 MILE
VARSITY START

CEMETERY HILL

1 M (V)

188 yds.

3 MILE H.S. &
FRESHMAN START

3 M (V)

2.5 mile H.S.
FINISH

THE FLATS

405 YARDS

VAN CORTLANDT
GOLF COURSE

FINISH
V and F

BROADWAY

SERVICE ROAD

approx. 440 yards to "cowpath"

½ M (F)

½ M (V)

START H.S.
2.5 MILE COURSE

BROADWAY

designed by Larry Byrne

They also annually run "The Mets," "The Heps," and the season's big attraction, the IC4A meet. In 1968, the NCAA, AAU and USTFF Nationals were held there in the same week. The NCAA returned to Van Cortlandt the following year as well.

Then, there is the "open" schedule sponsored by the local AAU or Road Runners Club (the nation's largest RRC chapter with more than 5000 members). Their events usually go off on Sundays. Some of them are age-group contests. The Age-Group Nationals is another annual feature. Masters events are held, and there are some races only for girls, such as the series sponsored by the Colgate-Palmolive Company. There is hardly a daylight hour on a fall weekend when a race is not in progress.

But Van Cortlandt is not only for racing. Many teams practice there, and the turf is pounded year round by runners and joggers of every description.

The high schools run 2.5 miles. They string behind a chalked line 200 strong and gaze at the clustered hills concealed by tall trees. A starter stands 50 yards in front of them. The pistol fires. They run for about 500 yards across the opening flats, which consist of several makeshift baseball fields on which are also played soccer, rugby and cricket. On the flats, runners must dodge baseball backstops, stray baby carriages and catcalls in a foreign tongue from the soccer players. A wedge is formed as though it was a swim race in which the fastest competitors were placed in the middle and the slowest were put on the ends.

The field is a minute into the race, charging like cavalry troops to the cowpath, a sand-filled stretch that is riveted with crevices and large boulders that peek through the ground like icebergs and are just as dangerous to the runners. Spectators frequent this spot, for it is also close to the finish line. They form narrow parallel lines, preventing the field from running more than five or six abreast. Coaches preach to their harriers: "Get out there. You gotta get out fast!" To the right is a fenced-off golf course. A few hundred yards later, the runners reach the base of the uphill section.

They climb a short, steep hill and hit the bridge, another spectator haunt. By this time, a good half-mile out, the pack has thinned considerably, and the onlookers can accurately identify runners by name or team. Over the bridge and into the hills. The tight paths are flanked by dense woods and coated with fallen leaves of many colors, making footing difficult. It is hard to make up ground; there is little room. The route is poorly marked except for the graffiti that has been painted on trees and boulders over the years. This is known as the Back Woods.

After the ascent, the runners cross a thin paved strip, signifying the start of the downhills. Halfway home. The veteran will not make the mistake of being too reckless on the descent. The terrain changes abruptly, big stones are evident everywhere, and there are plenty of turns. In rainy weather, watch out! One turn, Roller Derby Turn, is cornered at a 90-degree angle and is braced by a protective fence overlooking a big drop.

A short hill precedes the picnic grounds. A half-mile to go. The runners are then forced to hit pavement for 50 yards, and the clicking chorus of decelerating spikes alerts the strategically-positioned fans and coaches to their presence. Back over the bridge and flying down a steep, turf-churned hill, where a guard-fence was installed to prevent a possible tragedy with the adjacent highway traffic.

"I had a helluva job getting them to put up that fence," recalls a meet official. "I had to argue with the Parks Department. After they did, I sent them a note. It was probably the first thank-you letter they ever got."

Out of the hills and onto the final flats, a gravel path like the old baseball warning tracks. It is like coming out of the darkness and into the light. The sun hits you first, then the vastness of the flat fields where football peewees in helmeted uniforms drill and knock heads.

Here, there are two arrows. One says, "College" and points to the right, indicating the college finish. The other says "High School" and points left. They are not conspicuous. Many a novice runner has missed them.

Here we go. All you got left, man, right to the finish. The gravel feels good underfoot. Finally, the figures of partisan devotees appear larger. Push a little more, baby, and you're home. A marshall stands at the mouth of the chute, directing the finishing runners and admonishing those in the crowd who duck under the police barriers and onto the course. The exhausted runners comfort one another in the roped-off chute and are moved out of it quickly.

Mission accomplished.

When the New York State meet is held there, the high schoolers run three miles. A half-mile of flats is added to the 2.5. It is the same college freshman route used years ago before the NCAA permitted freshmen to become members of varsity teams. There is also an abbreviated course for high school freshmen and some levels of girls' competition. This is a 1.25- or 1.5-mile circuit that entirely bypasses the Back Woods.

The basic college course is five miles. They start on the meadow near the main rugby field on a line that, if extended, would run perpendicular to the final high school straightaway. They run the flats in a triangular fashion, cutting sharply to the left at two flagpoles and proceeding to the hills. When they reach the cowpath, the collegians are about one mile from the start. The leaders in the hot races like the IC4A reach this point in about 4:20.

They follow the high school trails in the hills, and when they emerge they bear right toward the college finish. They hit three miles about a hundred yards before that finish. The fastest splits hover not much above 14 minutes.

The two-mile loop remains. The initial flats are repeated. Along the cowpath, a sharp left like a detour is taken, up toward the infamous Cemetery Hill, a steep, rocky incline about 4.2 miles into the college run.

Cemetery—that's the way it's usually referred to, just "Cemetery"—rises about a hundred feet during its length of about 300 yards. Its peak stands 150 feet above sea level. It's a killer, alright, and the jibes abound. Runners die up there. They're dead and buried, laid to rest. Its name is so perfectly suited for the cross-country assignment that one would assume running there had some historical relationship to it. Not so.

Cemetery Hill was once known as Vault Hill. It is the family burial plot of the Van Cortlandts, the wealthy Dutch settlers after whom the park is named. In 1776, after the Revolutionary Battle of Long Island, Augustus Van Cortlandt, then the recording clerk for the City of New York, hid the city records from the British in a vault buried there. The records were later rehidden in Manhattan.

Five years later, in 1781, General George Washington kept campfires burning on the hill as a decoy for several days. He wanted the British to believe his forces were camping there while he withdrew his troops across the Hudson to march on Yorktown. I wonder if soldiers did any running on the way.

Cemetery slopes down to the bridge crossover, but the runners do not cross it again. They take a sharp left off the final downhill and head for home along the gravel straights that border Broadway. This is the same Broadway of theatres and street hustling 10 miles to the South in midtown Manhattan. Spectators line the small, grassy embankment that protrudes to the park's sidewalk edge, and they can almost touch the harriers as they stride anxiously into the narrow chute. It has been a day's work.

When the colleges run six miles, as they did for the NCAA in 1968 and 1969, the runners do two laps of the three-mile route, bypassing Cemetery Hill. For 10,000 meters, as in the 1968 AAU, the start is moved back toward upper Broadway, and then the six-mile course is tackled.

What a show that was in '68. Van Cortlandtites could savor the annual IC4A—plus the AAU, NCAA and USTFF Nationals. The four meets were packaged in 13 days in November, and that's all anyone at the park spoke about in October. It was an unlucky 13 for the I.C.'s, for the race was belted with a huge downpower, not an uncommon setting there. *Track and Field News* described the course as "resembling a five-mile strip through the Mekong Delta."

The weather held up for the latter meets. I remember cutting college classes to attend the NCAA, held as usual on the Monday before Thanksgiving. A lot of other people cut classes, took sick days at work and rearranged their schedules to absorb the atmosphere of an NCAA at Vanny. I loved the unfamiliar uniforms from Minnesota, Colorado and Drake, and even more so the following year when the NCAA returned and the bright yellow and green of Oregon appeared.

"There's Pre!" someone shouted. "And Lindgren!" The best part was before the race when any kid could approach the name runners and watch them warm up and gesture, or take their pictures or even talk to them. The Prefontaines and Lindgrens were suddenly real, not just names in the paper, and their mannerisms were open for public view.

The Van Cortlandt faithful were not disappointed. Their favorites, the Irishmen of Villanova, won three championships (they didn't enter the USTFF). This invigorated the post-race merriment at the local bars and displaced the exalted references to Bob Beamon's Olympic long jump title. Beamon was not long out of Jamaica High in Queens when in Mexico City he popped 29 feet 2-1/2 inches (8.90 meters as the crow flies), widely regarded as the single greatest achievement in track and field history.

Both the high school and college routes have gone through many revisions over the years since cross-country came to Van Cortlandt Park at the turn of the century. The evolution of the current courses reflect the alterations to the park as a whole.

"As far as I know, there weren't any races run here before 1900," recalls one old-timer. "Back in those days, they ran through what is now the golf course. At one point, the runners had to cross a water jump, one that couldn't be crossed without getting wet. It ran about six miles."

Larry Byrne is a leading New York track official and master statistician who put in a long hitch in the Marines in the 1950s and early '60s that interrupted his 25-year association with Van Cortlandt. Larry's love for statistics is fueled by his uncanny memory, which has lodged in it blueprints of the old Van Cortlandt routes.

"In the late '40s," he says, "the college course finished in the stadium. (There is a small stadium, built in 1934, that houses a cinder track.) The runners came through an open gate at the end of the old 220-yard straightaway, made a turn onto the curve of the track and ran in the *opposite* direction (clockwise), in effect facing the incoming runners who had yet to circle the track."

The *1949 IC4A Handbook* has pictures showing Rhode Island's Robert Black winning the 1947 and 1948 events at the on-the-track finish line. I am almost sure I recognize in the photo officials and spectators who still show up at Van Cortlandt today.

Byrne ran for Brooklyn Prep Academy in those days. He relates that the high school teams started on a plane perpendicular to the current start, their backs to Broadway. They used the same final straight as did the colleges, because the trestle of a train route extended past what is now the high school finish. It seems a suburban spur of the New York Central Railroad that got rolling at Grand Central Station was routed through Van Cortlandt before heading up to Yonkers.

Byrne, a self-confessed "railroad freak," claims this line was suspended on June 30, 1943, but the trestle remained for a number of years thereafter. Runners approaching the cowpath had to avoid smacking into the support poles for the tracks, which were about 15 or 20 feet high, according to Byrne. Today, the remaining evidence of the train's intrusion is a thin bridge over which the train went after leaving the area of the course. (This is not the same bridge used by the runners.)

Moreover, years ago the high school course was 2.25 miles. It was lengthened to 2.5, but a remeasurement in 1960 revealed it to be a bit less than that distance. Thus, the finish was moved about 60 yards, and the old records were revised.

Normally, cross-country times have little significance per se; it is the place and team finish that count. But the volume of running at Van Cortlandt has given added meaning to the performances there. There are two main barriers. High schoolers try to break 13 minutes for the 2.5, collegians try to break 25 minutes for the five miles. Through the 1976 campaign, 241 harriers had achieved the former, starting with William Leahy of Boston's Catholic Memorial High, who did it in a small meet in 1963. More than 100 collegians have broken 25 flat.

These figures were compiled by Byrne and Walt Krolman, assistant coach at St. John's University.

The high school record of 12:16.4 was set in 1975 by Luis Ostolozaga of Bishop Loughlin, Brooklyn, also in a small conference meet when a strong, determined youngster can free himself from the anxieties of meeting equally strong runners and congested fields. Ostolozaga, whose name was regularly misspelled in the New York newspapers, enrolled at Manhattan College, the neighborhood school situated in fashionable Riverdale, less than a mile away from the Van Cortlandt starting line.

Only 16 runners have bettered 12:30, which is a pace of five minutes per mile. This sort of pace is recorded with regularity at other, less challenging high school domains. Very few scholastic squads can get close to a 13-minute average for their five scoring runners. In 1971, a group from St. Joseph's High in Buffalo, accomplished what was though to be impossible. This finely tuned unit raced to an average of 12:53.5, a mark bettered at the time by only 40 or so individuals from among the many thousands who had competed there. This team was surely one of the finest ever assembled at Van Cortlandt, and its coach, Bob Ivory, (now retired), is still glowing from the tributes that group received.

Cross-country addicts love to speculate about the times that world-class runners could achieve on the high school course. What could Gerry Lindgren have done in his prime? (He ran five-minute pace for six miles while winning the 1969 NCAA there. A conservative estimate would put him near 12 minutes even at only 2.5.) What about the Africans, like a Ben Jipcho or Kip Keino, or the latest harrier hero, 1976 NCAA champion Henry Rono? Under 12 minutes is usually the consensus. Gasp!

One schoolboy who was thought to have a chance to approach 12 minutes flat was Denis Fikes. Fikes ran for Rice High of Manhattan and as a sophomore in 1967 won the Catholic league title in 12:50. He was a gangling youth, awkward in style and not known for a particularly heavy training regimen. "Wait till his senior year," declared his followers, shaking their heads. Fikes continued to win but never got below 12:25.7, then 2.4 seconds off the course record put down in 1966 by Marty Liquori.

Perhaps Fikes, at 6'4", was too tall to move with excessive speed and efficiency through the unpredictable trails. However, his record of 16 victories in 20 large-scale starts over three seasons remains the most enviable teenage composite ever seen in those parts. Later, as a Marine, he would run a 3:55 mile.

Liquori attended Essex Catholic High in Newark and became the most heralded runner to come out of Van Cortlandt since the course became an exact 2.5 in 1960. In the spring of '67, he ran a sensational 3:59 mile (still second only to Jim Ryun's scholastic 3:55.3) and went on to further laurels at Villanova. His Olympic fortunes have been misfortunes, but I think he could stake a successful claim in the 10,000 in 1980, should he find adequate training time amid his expanding business interests.

The five-mile college record is 23:51, run by Pennsylvania's Dave Merrick in the 1975 IC4A race. The most prominent runner to grace the trails in recent years was Frank Shorter, the 1972 Olympic marathon champion. Frank's best time was 24:52 when he was runner-up in the 1968 Heptagonal meet.

One of the finest harriers ever to rise from the Van Cortlandt dust was Matt Centrowitz, who ran marvelously in the early '70s for Power Memorial Academy, situated near Lincoln Center and coached by a rare jewel of a Christian Brother, J. Gregory Bielen. (Brother Bielen recently accepted an assignment as principal of a Rhode Island Catholic school.)

Centrowitz transferred his talent within the local family by going on to Manhattan College and running 24:21, a college freshman record for the five-mile route. But he had certain difficulties at Manhattan, one being the demanding indoor track schedule indigenous to the East. After his freshman year, Matt packed up and went out to the University of Oregon, which does not maintain an active indoor campaign. What it does maintain is the finest distance running environment in the United States, and that speaks also for cross-country.

It was ironic, then, that Matt would falter in cross-country. With such an extraordinary crop of distance runners, Matt's cross-country skills were suddenly expendable, and besides he and Oregon Coach Bill Dellinger saw his ultimate talents elsewhere, in the one-mile run. In 1973, Matt had been the leading US schoolboy in that event, having done 4:02.7. In 1976, he made the US Olympic team in the 1500 meters and ran the equivalent of a 3:53 mile. That was all Matt wanted.

The IC4A meet is the annual World Series of Van Cortlandt, when close to a hundred Eastern colleges and a few from the Midwest and South gather at the park for a cross-country festival of excitement and duress. There are two competitions, one for the runners and one for the spectators who form a dense boundary along the finish embankment and park themselves ingeniously at vantage points in the hills. Without building up too much of a sweat, it is possible to see the field at the start, at one mile, three miles and at the finish. Energetic viewers can also grab one or two other peeks.

There had been 69 of these affairs from 1908 through 1977. It was not held in 1918 because of World War I. Curiously, there were no interruptions during World War II. Even the World Series and Olympic Games stopped for that.

The IC4A was first held in Princeton, N.J., and had four other sites in Massachusetts, New York and Connecticut before settling down for good at Van Cortlandt in 1916.

There have been three distinct eras. In the early years, Cornell won nine titles in a 14-year span. From '32 to '61, Michigan State, the nation's cross-country power, captured 13 trophies. Then, Villanova's Wildcats won seven of 10, including a record six straight.

Four runners have won three titles in a row: John Paul Jones of Cornell (1910-12), Leslie MacMitchell of NYU (1939-41), Richard Shea of Army (1949-51) and Crawford Kennedy of Michigan State (1957-59). Crawford inherited the title from his brother Henry, who triumphed in 1955 and 1956, giving the Kennedy family five straight.

The team champion has had the individual winner in 26 of the 68 races, a rather high 38%. Lehigh has captured six small-schools ("College Division") races in eight years (1969-76) since this section began in 1962.

One of the more memorable IC4A races came in 1974. The race was filled with accomplished runners, but they had the bite taken out of them by Dennis Trujillo of West Point by way of Pueblo, Colo. Trujillo dashed out quickly, at an almost reckless pace and acquired a large early lead. It worked. Nobody could catch him and he hung on for a smart victory. Trujillo, all of 5'8" and 135 pounds, could not even run the NCAA the following week. His reward was a dual-meet assignment with Navy.

Teamwise, Massachusetts won the Battle of the Bronx which experts thought would go to unbeaten Georgetown or Providence. Only 36 points separated the first five teams. The contenders had to loiter at the finish for what seemed an eternity while the Manhattan College computers sorted out the places.

"We were thinking IC4A all year," said an emotionally drained Ken O'Brien, the U-Mass coach, in tears after the tally was in.

My favorite IC4A moment came before a race. It was 1975. The college starting line borders a large area frequented by rugby players. Rugby players are not negotiators. They hit first and ask questions later. So when the harriers took their marks for the start, and the rugby men refused to halt their game even briefly, words were exchanged and a couple of guys got belted. And they weren't rugby players.

This was not my favorite part. I enjoyed what ensued. Bob Hersh intervened.

Bob is a meticulous, hard-working, literate man in his late 30s with an Ivy League assurance to his manner and speech. He went to Columbia and the Harvard Law School, and is a respected Manhattan attorney. He is also one of the world's leading track and field authorities. Bob uses his vacation time to travel the country and the world to watch and report on track meets. He does a lot of work as a labor of love for *Track & Field News* and is the public address announcer at winter meets in Madison Square Garden. He is a stickler for minutia and esoterica, and knows both the rule book and the record book inside and out.

Bob takes a lot of good-natured kidding, mostly from within his circle of Eastern track authorities. We like to joke that nothing in track can ever really be taken as accurate unless Bob Hersh has given his official stamp of approval. Bob enhances his reputation every April at the Penn Relays before a pressbox full of friends and colleagues. Penn does a remarkably efficient job of running the world's largest outdoor track meet. Yet one hears Hersh, every hour on the hour, steaming with disapproval over one technicality or another. We love it—and him. We call him "The Guru."

So here he was in a three-piece pinstripe suit and wearing several stopwatches as a general wears his medals, standing face-to-face with striped-shirted rugby players and trying to be logical. With just the right blend of tact, authority and, I suppose, logic, he convinced the ruffians to let the gun go off and send the runners out on their appointed rounds. But for a while, it was touch and go.

Famous names and famous races have been but a part of the fabric of Van Cortlandt, whose ambiance on fall weekends is a microcosm of the entire town. There is an overlapping tapestry; no one has a place just for himself. Soccer and football and baseball and rugby and cricket mesh on the wide-open flats, and players of different skins shout instructions in many languages. There is golf to the east and the track stadium to the south and tennis courts that are no longer vacant and a new indoor swim complex. There is a riding stable in the hills, and people stroll across all territory to reach the picnic grounds.

Runners are everywhere—warming up, training, racing, going off in all directions or waiting at the one restroom or finding their own in the woods, patronizing the soft-drink vendors or the delis or the burger palace. There are rows of cars and buses near the entrance. It is a place of continuous movement that embodies the spirit of New York.

While the records for racing and pacing are made out in the hills, the record for beer consumption is registered at the Dutchman's, a bar and hamburger joint across from the park on Broadway. Its marquee may read Terminal Bar & Grill, situated as it is at the subway's end, but to the cross-country faithful it is the Dutchman's. (Its previous owners were Dutch.) Race scoring is often done there, especially when it rains. Meetings are held there. So are post-race celebrations. It is a lasting landmark. And it better not relocate, because the harriers—or at least their coaches—would have to relocate the races as well.

A place is only as good as its stories, and Van Cortlandt lore is well stocked with truth and exaggeration. A half-century ago, Joe McClusky of Fordham, 1932 Olympic bronze medalist in the steeplechase, arrived late for a race and watched the field take off on the course. He hurriedly stripped down and chased after it. He won. McClusky, nearing 70, still runs and usually wins the handicapped Met League alumni race, at which times are adjusted based on year of graduation.

On many occasions, teams have been disqualified; sometimes the reason has been course-cutting, inadvertent or intentional. In one instance, a high school unit was quite bold in its affront to the rules. During the race, the team ran to the bridge crossover and stopped with the hope of not being noticed. When the field came out of the hills and across the bridge the second time, toward the finish, the rested team joined the leaders for the final kick.

With high school and college events running concurrently, there has been the problem of two distinct racing fields merging onto the same paths. Inevitably, the smaller college fields suffer—from claustrophobia.

A classic case occurred in 1974. It was the City University race, among non-scholarship runners, and a revitalized Baruch College team was making a bid under its new coach, Roy Chernock. Chernock has been awarded four international coaching assignments by US officials—and not for being a house man. He is notably outspoken. He also has a way of making miracles out of mediocrity. After a 10-1 dual-meet slate, Baruch went into the CUNY race with confidence. But a schoolboy field pulled up to the cowpath at an inconvenient moment. "They ran into us and wiped us out," said Chernock. Baruch placed second—

by one point.

Dr. Emory Szanto, a physician, is another Van Cortlandt mainstay. Affixed with a permanent smile, he roams the meadow imparting philosophy with a nasal voice to anyone who will listen. He pokes you with an index finger to get your attention. He is kidded about his alleged reliance on cortisone to cure the world's injuries. Often, he is the official meet doctor, treating spiked heels and battered egos. On one clear Saturday, a runner who had just completed his race was stung by a bee on his tongue, which swelled enormously, endangering his life. Dr. Szanto quickly came to his aid and reduced the swelling, saving him.

An aging gentleman named Charley Westerholm appeared at Van Cortlandt every September until his death in 1977 and cleared debris that accumulates on the racing route during the off-season. I was often told of this man but did not take the story seriously until I had reason to interview a runner at a pre-season practice and saw Charley removing sharp-edged rocks from the cowpath.

Westerholm could have worked day and night and never removed half of the debris, which even though hazardous enables the circuit to more closely resemble the rugged European courses. At times, it comes very close. Rain lubricates the course and makes footing treacherous. The wind knocks over trees which fall across the narrow trails, forcing runners to hurdle them. Mischievous kids perched on heavy branches have been seen tossing small stones with abandon.

The greatest indignancy has been the conflict, somewhat abated now, with the horseback riders. Following is a condensation of a feature story I wrote a few years ago for *The New York Times*. It was headlined:

Riders, Runners Try to Bridge a Compatibility Gap

Scholastic cross-country runners who use Van Cortlandt Park on fall weekends have more than steep hills to contend with. Horses are disputing their right of way.

Horseback riders, disturbed at the presence of the runners—who number almost 3000 on some Saturdays—threaten the races in general and the athletes in particular.

The conflict is centered on a short bridge overlooking the Henry Hudson Parkway that connects the northern section of the Bronx park, which borders on Westchester County. About a half-mile from the start of the 2½-mile high school races, the bridge intersects the bridle path used by the Van Cortlandt Park riding stables.

At this spot, packs of harriers, five and six abreast, run across the bridge. They are often met by irate riders who claim the sole right of the path that crosses the bridge. The school leagues claim rights by virtue of a Parks Department permit, which must be obtained to conduct a meet.

Many coaches and officials complained that riders interfere with the races by intimidating the runners and forcing them off the course in the area of the bridge. There have also been incidents of injury to runners allegedly caused by riders on horseback. Some were said to have been intentional.

The most recent incident occurred on Oct. 23 in the Fordham University Eastern States Championship meet. Horses were ridden across the path just as runners passed by, causing many athletes to stumble, and at least one athlete, Vince Cartier of Scotch Plains, N.J., to stop. Cartier, the pre-meet favorite, finished 24th.

Bob Gregorio, who has worked for the riding stable for 17 years and became its owner a month ago, said, "I can't make a living. The riders come back and tell me they can't get through (the trails). These coaches are playing games with these races. For me, it's a living.

"The runners are scaring my horses. I've told my instructors, 'If they get in your way, knock 'em down!'"

Marty Lewis, South Shore coach and chairman of track and cross-country for the Public Schools Athletic League, recalled an incident a few years ago when a runner was actually picked up by an experienced rider and tossed off the course. The incidents have not been isolated.

Joe Fox, director of track and cross-coutnry for the Catholic High Schools Athletic Association, said the Police Department and Parks Department have been notified of the incidents on several occasions.

"But," said Fox, "the horses are still there."

Gregorio's complaint extended beyond the runners. He said his riders "are threatened by muggers, rapists and sexual perverts" as they travel his 15 miles of trails. "This place is worse than Central Park."

Meet officials would also like to see more police at the park to prevent clashes with horseback riders and to apprehend "hooligans" who sometimes block racing paths or throw rocks at the runners.

One observer remarked philosophically, "The problem's not only the horses. It's what they leave behind."

For Marty Lewis, the horse confrontations were topped for anxiety by an incident in 1965 when he coached Louis Brandeis High to its third city public schools title in four years.

"I was having practice," recalls Marty, "with some youngsters I had seen at school and had asked to try out. I told them to jog the course with some experienced boys. The experienced kids ran ahead of them. Finally, the young kids—they were only freshmen—found their way back to the start. But when we were all ready to leave, I noticed *one* pile of books still sitting there. It was already 6:30.

"We went up into the hills looking for this kid. He was nowhere. We asked other runners if they spotted him. No luck. Even a cop on a scooter couldn't find him. We were panic-stricken. Finally, at about 8 o'clock, he came jogging out of the hills. It was dark, and he had strayed up to Yonkers. I almost shit in my pants. Y'know what he said to me? 'This sport ain't for me.'"

Lewis feared the worst. The worst did happen to Robert Byrne, a Fordham University senior, out for a typical practice run in the fall of '75. Bobby was found dead on the course, with no bruises. He had run for several years and was in superb condition. An autopsy did not reveal the cause of death, according to a Fordham official close to the situation. "It's still a mystery," he said. Byrne's coach and teammates wore black armbands for the rest of the season.

Who were the Van Cortlandts anyway?

Oloff Van Cortlandt, a Dutchman, arrived in New Amsterdam in 1638 and founded a dynasty which at one time owned about 200 square miles of land. This land, formerly a Mohegan Indian hunting and planting ground, was purchased for a small sum from the British settlers. The Van Cortlandts were traders, merchants and shipbuilders, and they married into such families as the Schuylers, Philipses and Livingstons, thus doubling their wealth and influence.

Oloff's son, Stephanus, was appointed mayor in 1677, the first native-born American to hold that post. He purchased a large parcel of land from the Indians for wampum that included six tobacco boxes, six earthen jugs, one small coat, nine blankets and 14 kettles. Part of this bargain included what is now the 1146-acre Van Cortlandt Park. Perhaps cross-country entry fees should be paid in tobacco boxes to commemorate the purchase.

In 1748, Oloff's grandson, Frederick, built the family mansion, which still stands near the high school starting line. "It was a handsome manor, almost square, built of rogun fieldstone with fine brick trim around the windows," according to New York City historians Harmon H. Goldstone and Martha Dalrymple. Today's cowpath was really a path for cows. The family farmed the land and lived in the house until 1889 when they donated the property to the city for use as a public park.

The Van Cortlandt mansion served briefly as a police station until 1896 when it was placed in the custody of the National Society of Colonial Dames of the State of New York, which now maintains it as a museum. It was at this time that athletic-minded men gravitated to the park's trails.

The flats were used as camping grounds during the Revolutionary War and World War I. Washington used the Van Cortlandt estate as his headquarters at various times. During World War I, the site was used as a training area. The doughboys dug trenches, hiked through the woods, did combat training, and prepared themselves for the campaign against the Axis powers in France.

Combat still goes on there, only the intentions are less lethal. Let's hope it stays that way.

7
US Nationals

In 1968, Gerry Lindgren, a running veteran at age 22, did not enter the NCAA Cross-Country Championships in New York City. He passed up the entire fall season, not wanting to fool with the injuries that prevented him from making the US Olympic team.

In 1972, Steve Prefontaine, who was to meet his tragic death three years later, did not enter the NCAA Championships in Houston. He, too, skirted the fall campaign in the aftermath of his fourth place in the Olympic 5000 in Munich two months before.

Had these quadrennial digressions not interfered, Lindgren and Prefontaine, the glamor boys of the American distance running Renaissance, may very well have recorded back-to-back three-year sweeps of the NCAA title.

The NCAA. The Nationals. The "NC2A," some call it. Call it what you will, it is America's premier cross-country run. It is not the largest or the oldest, but it is the most colorful and the most important—the one every collegian aspires to, and, in these days, a race of international stature. Unlike the AAU, which celebrated its golden anniversary when the NCAA was just getting started, the Nationals also features a team

70

fight of great seriousness and has an elaborate qualifying system that causes coaches to plot and predict well before the summer sun fades away.

"The NCAA" is actually one of three NCAA groups. It is Division I, the same NCAA that in March has the nation hopping with its basketball championship. All those TV-contracted football teams are in this division. It is the Big One, "major" college, at least in terms of sports glory.

There are also NCAA II and III, not to mention the AAU, NAIA, JUCO, AIAW, USTFF and the RRC. It is the alphabet soup of amateur—quasi-amateur?—athletics, and in the fall of 1977 these organizations would crown more than 50 national cross-country champions. Their races would transpire in a period of a few weeks, for boys and girls and men and women of all ages who would run from one mile to 10,000 meters.

For most of these events, there is no fancy qualifying system. Just be of a certain age or sex and be at the right place at the right time, and you're in. Now, being at the right place at the right time has somewhat of a selective effect, because the Eastern runner hoping to compete in a California-scheduled AAU has to come up with $400 airfare and other travel expenses, unless he is renowned enough for his affiliated club to invest in his entry.

Speaking of the AAU, for years I had assumed that not just anyone could enter. There *had* to be some qualifying curtain. I mean, how would it look if a slowpoke like me stripped off a pair of Army-Navy store sweats and threw it in a pile next to Marty Liquori's? When I discovered that AAU membership was the only requirement, I set my sights on the 1976 run contested in Bicentennial Philadelphia. Me in the National AAU! I was already contemplating the great story I would write about it when an injury forced me to put my plans in abeyance. With the 1977 event in Houston, I didn't know when my next shot would be. So Liquori could relax.

LINDGREN

Gerry Lindgren shocked the track world in 1964. At a time when the high school indoor record for two miles was 9:23.5, the Spokane, Wash., teenager ran nine minutes flat. Then 8:46. Then 8:40. The 8:40 is still the best ever run by a US schoolboy, indoors or out.

In running circles, conversants dwelled upon Lindgren's astonishing trail of performances. He was 5'6", 120 pounds and 17 years old. He appeared younger ᴗnd looked the stereotype of the gosh-golly-gee-whiz

71

paperboy of TV situation comedies. I always thought there was a striking resemblance between Lindgren and Jerry Mathers, the Beaver on "Leave It To Beaver."

Gerry's paperboy image is not without foundation. In junior high, Lindgren had a paper route that took him through the Spokane streets for five miles. He ran it. One pictures that as a facsimile of an interval workout: running fast, stopping to deliver a paper and repeating the process many times.

After the 8:40 two-mile, Gerry announced he would run the AAU three-mile in New York's Madison Square Garden against Australia's Ron Clarke, the world's greatest distance runner. I recall sitting in the stands of the "old" Garden with friends and watching the elf-like Lindgren prance about. He tossed a pile of snow in the air, which the P.A. announcer said was imported from Spokane. The photographers, and the crowd, loved it.

Lindgren went out and placed third in a scholastic record of 13:37.8 (he did 13:17 outdoors), one of the world's best indoor three-miles. Clarke won it in 13:18.4 for a new world record. In a Mutt-'n'-Jeff tandem, the stately Clarke and pixyish Lindgren embraced around the waist and jogged a victory lap.

That summer, Lindgren put the crowning jewel on his scholastic career. He won the 10,000 in the US-Soviet dual meet before a screaming crowd at the Los Angeles Coliseum, a national-TV audience and a media obsessed with "beating the Russians." (The US did win, 139-97.)

Reported *Track & Field News:* "Lindgren, the 18-year-old baby of the team, stole the hearts of the sun-drenched spectators as he bided his time in the 10,000 for 3-1/2 miles before shooting past the Russian competitors to win by 120 yards."

Lindgren went on to the 1964 Olympics, Washington State, 14 national titles, several records, adulthood, several injuries and retirement. If things had been different in Gerry's youth, he might have become an outstanding marathoner. But his 200-mile-per-week training load took its toll.

In 1968, he was fourth in the Olympic Trials 5000, just missing a second berth on the US team. He laid low the rest of the year, missing an almost certain third straight NCAA cross-country title that fall. He returned to cross-country in 1969 and won another NCAA title.

After the race, he told reporter Jim Dunaway, "I was scared, really scared, so I wanted to lead all the way. I didn't look back at all. I was afraid I might see somebody gaining on me."

PREFONTAINE

He would have seen Steve Prefontaine, an Oregon freshman, whose heroics were being compared with Lindgren's at every opportunity. Pre was also from the Northwest, from the coastal town of Coos Bay, Ore. He also produced a phenomenal set of performances, including a prep outdoor two-mile (8:41.6) record and a 13:52.8 5000 on a European tour. Steve's overseas roommate? Gerry Lindgren.

The comparisons stop with appearance. Pre was taller, heavier, more muscular. He was rugged and cocky. He ran from the top: you noticed the strength of his arms, the squared shoulders and chest.

In the late '60s and early '70s, Lindgren and Prefontaine personified the rise of US distance running, and their successes in the collegiate cross-country Nationals were the cornerstones of that era. By 1975, Lindgren's career was over; Pre's was reaching its zenith, with an impending Olympic gold medal bid. But in the early hours of May 30, Steve Roland Prefontaine was killed in a one-car collision on a wooded hillside street in Eugene.

The *Track & Field News* obituary read:

"He apparently lost control of his small sports car rounding a sharp curve, crossed the center-line, struck a rock wall and flipped over several times. He apparently died instantly, although autopsy reports indicate his injuries (alone) wouldn't have proved fatal. Rather, he was suffocated by the weight of the convertible.

"Pre's death came as he returned from dropping off a friend and rival Frank Shorter at the home of a fellow runner Kenny Moore. All had earlier attended a party following the Oregon Twilight meet to honor the visiting Finnish Athletes."

The Oregon Twilight meet is now called the Prefontaine Classic.

NCAA HISTORY

The first NCAA run was held in 1938. Notre Dame's Greg Rice, a fine miler, won the race. Indiana took the team title. It was run on Michigan State's four-mile course in East Lansing and continued there until 1965, when the meet switched to Kansas and a six-mile route.

Michigan State made the most of its home-course advantage and dominated the meet for the first two decades. The Spartans won first in 1939 and added seven titles in a 12-year span under coach Karl Schlademan. Its only individual triumph came in 1958 when Crawford Kennedy won the trophy.

Besides Michigan State, the only teams to win three straight were Drake (1944-46), under coach Bill Easton, later renowned at Kansas, and Villanova (1966-68) for coach James "Jumbo" Elliot. Villanova, victorious again in 1970, would have notched five in a row if it could have erased a 14-point advantage held by triumphant Texas-El Paso in 1969. Similarly, Tennessee, in 1972, spoiled Oregon's bid. The Ducks would have beaten Tennessee if not for Pre's absence, and since they won the next two years they would have strung four in a row. Four seems to be the unattainable figure in NCAA competition. UTEP, however, captured the 1975 and 1976 affairs and with a returning crop of Kenyans with fertile eligibility, the Miners may reach the magic number.

The list of individual NCAA winners is sprinkled with accomplished champions and record-holders. Prefontaine and Lindgren. Gil Dodds, Fred Wilt, Wes Santee, Al Lawrence, Nick Rose. Interestingly, only one victor has won an Olympic medal—Lawrence, third in the '56 10,000. The last to try, Illinois' Craig Virgin, the 1975 winner, was sixth in his 10,000 heat and did not make the final at Montreal.

Another combination hard to come by is winning the NCAA and AAU titles in the same year. Few have even won both events in separate years. Same-year feats were achieved only by Robert Black (1948) and Lawrence (1959 and '60). Fred Wilt, author of the groundbreaking *Run, Run, Run*, gets the longevity award. He took the NCAA in '42 and the last of three AAU titles in '53. Lawrence's back-to-back doubles may never be topped in light of the reluctance of victorious collegians in recent years to run the AAU as well. Quit while you're ahead, is the rationale, I suppose. Ask Nick Rose. After taking the 1974 NCAA in Bloomington, Ind., he went out to California and ran the AAU. He placed 68th.

The recent team domination by Oregon and Villanova has not happened by accident. Oregon was coached by Bill Bowerman and now by Bill Dellinger, one of his former runners who won the 1964 Olympic bronze medal in the 5000 in Tokyo. Villanova has been headed by the aforementioned Jumbo Elliot. All three men have shown the ability to get fine, young athletes to trust their judgments and rely on their wisdom. This has been their common denominator.

Under Bowerman, Oregon became the supreme distance running school in America. It has produced more than a score of sub-four-minute milers and is exalted wherever track people meet. Bowerman pioneered many of the present-day running theories and training methods, and even designed and originated the waffle-soled shoes. Oregon has attracted recruits from near and far, from the three McChesney brothers of hometown Eugene to recently acclaimed schoolboys Rudy Chapa of Hammond, Ind., and Alberto Salazar of Wayland, Mass.

At a coaching clinic in 1972, Dellinger outlined The Oregon System, as initiated by Bowerman, in a 15-point program. The last point: "Running should be a way of life for runners."

Elliot also attracts runners from near and far—the near being Philadelphia and the Northeast, and the far being Ireland. Marty Liquori, from Cedar Grove, N.J., and Ron Delany, from Ireland, are but two examples. Characteristically, the Wildcats' 1966 NCAA championship squad had on it names like O'Leary, Donnelly, Murphy, Patrick, Hamilton and Messenger.

Coach Elliot is not very large, not in physique, to have been distinguished with the name Jumbo. Supposedly, he was in high school when the Philadelphia Phillies had a 235-pound pitcher named Jumbo Elliot. The name stuck.

Jumbo doesn't put in a full day at Villanova. Bob Hersh of *Track & Field News* explained it: "Every afternoon from September to June, at about the same hour that Clark Kent is excusing himself from the city room of the *Daily Planet* to tend his more glamorous second career, a similar transformation takes place in the Main Line suburbs of Philadelphia. There, business executive James F. Elliot of Elliot & Frantz, Inc., dealers in heavy equipment, puts down his briefcase, picks up his stopwatch and drives down the road to Villanova University, where he becomes 'Jumbo' Elliot, one of the nation's most successful track coaches."

In the 1976 NCAA meet, Villanova had one of its worst outings, placing 21st in a field of 34 teams, while Oregon finished a strong second. The Ducks, with five Americans—two from California and one each from Alaska, Indiana and the Bronx—scored 117. Texas-El Paso—with five Kenyans—won with 62 points. A lot of people didn't like that.

It was the same story in the race for the single gold medal. Craig Virgin, the defending champion, ran a marvelous race, but Washington State Kenyans Henry Rono and Samson Kimombwa ran away from him on the plains of the North Texas State golf course in Denton. Rono's winning time was 28:06.6, unheard of for 10,000-meter cross-country. Virgin was 130 yards back in 28:26. Kimombwa, second in 28:16, broke the world's esteemed 10,000-meter track record the next summer.

Rono, from the town of Kalenjum, in the Rift Valley section of Kenya, never heard of Virgin—or of Texas. He raced with imprudent irreverence, hitting three miles in 13:27 and getting away with it. He manipulated Virgin, who was both bitter and awestruck.

Said Craig, "They don't even know how old they are. It takes years to develop that much endurance. Their age is too much. . . . I thought they were bluffing, but they showed no sign of weakness. I never dreamed cross-country could be that fast."

A lot of people didn't like that either. No sir. Virgin and Oregon—our US heroes—could not even get close to the Africans. That's what seemed to be underlying the disillusionment of ardent cross-country followers. It was like the US government sending its best astronauts to Mars only to have the Russians beat them there by a few light years.

Consequently, at the post-race awards ceremony, the applause was more obligatory than sincere when the victorious Kenyans were called into the spotlight to accept their prizes. The native Americans honored were given a rousing reception. Make no mistake about it: The sentiment was clearly "Us" against "Them."

The foreign influence, which now reaches its seasonal boiling point in the Nationals, goes back many years, even before the Irishmen of Villanova, to the victory by Houston in 1960. Led by Australian Olympian Al Lawrence, Houston scored 54 points with five non-Americans. And six of the first eight finishers were foreigners. So the patterns are not new; just the reactions to them.

The foreign pattern also was evident in 1972, when the South—actually the Border South—staked a successful claim on a muddy course in Houston. Tennessee won and East Tennessee State was second. The Vols had only one foreigner while East displayed its six-man Irish Brigade, led by gold medalist Neil Cusack, an Irish Olympian.

Cusack returned to the Nationals in 1973, his senior year, but so did Prefontaine for what was to be his cross-country swan song. Pre took his third NCAA title, outdueling Western Kentucky's Nick Rose on a scenic course in Spokane, Wash. Cusack was fourth. What a field! Wilson Waigwa was fifth, John Ngeno ninth and a freshman named Craig Virgin 10th.

After his win, Pre was encircled by youthful admirers, some wearing "Go-Pre" T-shirts. "Of my three wins," he said, "I'd call this one the toughest, due to the competition, weather and everything put together. I've never seen a guy [Rose] that far ahead of me in a cross-country race. But with a half-mile to go, I knew he couldn't stay with me."

MORE "NATIONALS"

In 1958, the NCAA established a national cross-country championship for its College Division level. The division had national contests at the time in only one other sport, basketball. This small-schools league held its annual run in Wheaton, Ill., until 1974, when it switched to a rotation basis and moved to Springfield, Mo. The College Division race grew from 16 schools and 82 athletes in 1958 to 84 schools (not all full teams) and 413 athletes in 1972, necessitating a further split into NCAA Division II and NCAA Division III. In 1973, both factions held their championships in Wheaton and separated to different sites the following year.

In NCAA II, San Diego State (now in Division I), put together three straight triumphs (1965-67) and averaged a remarkably low victory total of 60 points.The most significant single team performance came in 1971, still before the split, when victorious Fullerton State of California placed four runners in the top 10 in a field of 389. Fullerton scored 47. South Dakota State, with two-time (1973-74) champ Gary Bentley, maintains the best overall record of two victories and three seconds. On the move, though, is California State at Irvine, where a dynasty is brewing. The Anteaters—what a terrible team nickname— had the individual and team victors in 1975 and '76 and seemed headed for added trophies before they moved to Division I status.

There is an interesting collection of athletic obscurities in NCAA III, where academic achievement, not lush TV contracts, engender alumni pride. MIT, Brandeis, Case Western Reserve and Tufts are among its members. On the running front, the frontrunners have been North Central of Illinois, winner in 1975-76, and runnerup in 1973-74 when Ohio's Ashland and Mt. Union prevailed.

The NAIA runs go back to 1956. South Dakota State took the first title. While foreigners have won the last four individual awards, the team honors have been historically American. What is more American than Kansas? Fort Hays State and Emporia State have combined for eight victories and seven seconds, more or less dividing them. But only one of those 15 showings—a runnerup by Ft. Hays—came in the 1970s. In 1963 Emporia won both the NCAA II and NAIA, as did its champion runner John Camien. Camien, a great cross-country artist, is now coaching in the New York City suburbs of Long Island, not far from the schoolboy stomping grounds where he blossomed into a 4:10 teenage miler.

NAIA runners were put to a true cross-country test in 1965 when 25-degree temperatures, 14 miles per hour winds and a foot of snow hit the four-mile course in Omaha. Ft. Hays won by 74 points.

These two Kansas squads were coached by men of great stature. Ft. Hays' Alex Francis is in his 31st year at the institution. He has had many US international coaching assignments and in 1961 was coach of the South Vietnamese national team. Imagine South Vietnam with a track team, on the brink of the buildup of the Vietnam War.

Emporia's Fran Welch has been similarly honored in his 40-year tenure, which included coaching football for 24 seasons and a stint as athletic director. In 1960, he was a coach on the US Olympic squad in Rome. After his retirement in 1965, Welch continued to live in Emporia until his death a few years ago.

"Fran took great pride in the fact that he never had a track shoe on his foot, although he had a lot to do with the placement of the spikes for different types of runners," recalls Keith Caywood, current Emporia coordinator of athletics who preceded Welch as football coach in 1955.

USTFF

The USTFF has occupied an awkward place among American cross-country championships. Organized in 1962 as a result of the political haggling between the NCAA and AAU, the USTFF has systematically circulated its meet around the country. But the entries have been erratic and largely parochial.

In 1974, in Ann Arbor, Mich., Midwestern runners dominated the standings. In 1973, in San Diego, West Coast runners led the field. In 1972, in Texas, the Southwest controlled the action. In 1971, in Atlanta, the South rose to the occasion.

Part of the problem has been its late-November date, with the meet coming in the same week as the NCAA and AAU. To circumvent the congestion, the USTFF in 1976 held its meet in October for the first time. But the results still represented the locale. The site was Madison, Wis. Wisconsin won the team title, and Midwestern runners clogged the entry list.

Yet the victory stand has seen quite a spectrum of running artisans, from indoor mile hero Tom O'Hara (1963) to Holland's Arjan Helling (1967) to Olympic marathon champ Frank Shorter (1970). Tarry Harrison of Colorado State is the only two-time (1966-'68) victor.

St. John's of New York secured a place in history with a bit of luck in 1968. That fall, in a six-day period, the NCAA, USTFF and AAU all were held at Van Cortlandt Park in New York. The USTFF suffered mass defections, and the race was left with three full teams and a 52-man field. The Redmen beat Houston and NYU for the "championship."

JUNIOR COLLEGES

The junior colleges got under way with a national meet in 1959. Cobleskill of New York, the first winner, has won four times. Michigan has cornered the market on consistency. It has a very active JUCO association and has produced six team victories. Flint took one, Muskegan County two and Southwestern Michigan has three.

Southwestern, with the team nickname "Roadrunners," tied with Allegheny of Pittsburgh in 1973 and won the next two titles outright before Allegheny captured its own championship in 1976. After that victory, in Rochester, Minn., in 1975, Southwestern coach Ron Gunn said, "Our kids laid back and really worked those hills. All they saw the last mile was a blur. They were sore afterwards, but that's the way it should be."

Allegheny, which won more than 100 straight junior college dual meets since 1968, posted one of cross-country's all-time best performances in its 1976 triumph in Bethpage, N.Y. The Cougars put five runners in the top 10 for a record low point total of 18.

Coach Sam Bair said, "It still surprises me. I knew we were strong. We just hit it right."

Bair took over the head coaching reins from Neil Cohen, who retained his position of athletic director. Cohen, with exorbitant phone bills and energetic traveling, built a cross-country tradition at Allegheny, which competes favorably with four-year schools in attracting top Eastern schoolboys.

In 1975, Allegheny went farther East—to South Africa—and landed Robin Holland, who won the 1976 race. After Holland's initial cross-country victory in 1975, I wrote in *The Harrier:*

"Want to make a great movie?

"Take a 16-year-old boy and have him play soccer, cricket, rugby, field hockey and tennis. Then, have him run track and cross-country as a one-man team—without a coach. Set the show in South Africa and have him place third in the National Junior meet. Then fly him from the 6000-foot altitude of his homeland to the Texas Panhandle and, a few months later, to Pittsburgh, where he'll develop into a leading collegiate distance runner on a diet of seven-minute miles.

"Call it *The Robin Holland Story.*"

WOMEN

Women's cross-country is well-established in the AAU and AIAW spheres. The AAU story belongs to Doris Brown Heritage. She won five straight, from 1967 through '71, duplicating her more incredible string of International triumphs. In 1972, Francie Larrieu (sister of men's AAU champ Ron) halted her streak as Heritage placed second. Larrieu won again in 1973, then Lynn Bjorkland won twice and the reclusive Jan Merrill captured the '76 prize. Heritage, at 34, was still going strong in '76, placing fifth and proceeding to the Internationals.

The AIAW collegiate meet celebrates its fourth anniversary in 1977. Women's sports in Iowa is known for basketball clamor, but Iowa State has grabbed part of the spotlight by winning the first three AIAW titles. The University of Wisconsin at Madison hosted the 1976 event, and present were 23 full teams and 222 women representing 70 schools. Julie Brown of Cal State-Northridge, the AAU runnerup, won the three-mile race. This meet is in good health, indeed, and it is further testimony to the interest and ability of women in the field of distance running.

AAU

In contrast to the NCAA, the AAU races, started in 1890, have not been a jinx for Olympic aspirants. The most noteworthy champions were the Finns, Willie Ritola and Hannes Kolehmainen, not as revered but almost as extraordinary as their hallowed countryman, Paavo Nurmi.

Kolehmainen took the AAU in 1914, two years after winning the Olympic 5000 and 10,000 track events and the 8000-meter cross-country in Stockholm. He added the 1920 marathon in Antwerp to his collection. Ritola captured AAU races in 1922-23-25-27, and also collected three Olympic titles and two seconds (to Nurmi) in the 1924 and 1928 Games. Abel Kiviat of the US, 1912 AAU champ, was the 1500 runnerup in the 1912 Games, losing by one-tenth of a second. Horace Ashenfelter, three-time (1951, 1955-56) AAU titlist, won the 1952 Olympic steeplechase.

Don Lash of Indiana, the 1938 Sullivan Award winner as the nation's outstanding amateur athlete, is the all-time AAU leader with seven straight victories, from 1934 through 1940. In 1936, he ran for an Indiana University team that placed 1-2-3-4-5 to score a perfect 15 points. It is too bad the NCAA did not begin until 1938, for it would have been a treat to have had that sensational Indiana quintet in a national collegiate meet. Lash held many records and was known as an unselfish sportsman. Later, he worked as an agent for the Federal Bureau of Investigation.

Kolehmainen, although from Finland, represented the Irish-American Athletic Club, which won five team titles in the early years of the meet. Ritola ran for the Finnish-American AC, which acquired four titles in the '20s. New York's Millrose Athletic Association took over and pocketed 10 championships before the New York Athletic Club began its reign in 1940 with the first of 16 championships.

Not all winning clubs have had such conventional names. The 1976 champs were called the Jamul (pronounced HA-mul) Toads. They are coached by Bob Larsen, who took a ragtag assemblage called the Toads, added the name of a street near his San Diego home, Jamul, and came up with a smooth-running unit called the Jamul Toads. At last count, the team had only seven members, all champions in events ranging from the mile to the marathon and all natives of the San Diego area.

Four of the seven ran for Larsen at Grossmont Junior College in El Cajon, Calif. Larsen's cross-country teams there have won five straight state junior college titles in an area abundant in distance running talent. California schools are not part of the national junior college setup (nor are some Oregon and Washington schools), prompting thoughts as to how they could stand up against the latest teams from Southwestern Michigan or Allegheny.

Another AAU champion to win an Olympic title is Frank Shorter, who took four AAUs (1970-73) before a setback of 11th place in 1974. He was conspicuous by his absence in 1975 and 1976, for without him the tempo slowed, thereby altering race strategy and presumably the final placings. In recent years, Frank has given his allegiance more to the longer road runs and marathons, and because of his subdued demeanor and non-stop training he has become a sort of folk hero to thousands of running addicts across the country.

In '75, when Shorter was reportedly snow-trapped in Taos, N.M., where his parents live, none of the AAU contenders would go out on a limb and draft a fast pace. Thus, coming onto the homestretch of an oddly-devised Naval Academy course in Annapolis, there were still seven men in contention. Greg Fredericks, 1972 Penn State graduate, burst through the bunch and won by eight yards.

Of Shorter's triumphs, the 1972 race in Chicago was the toughest. Frank didn't cross the finish line first. NCAA champion Neil Cusack did, but was eventually placed fourth. Here is what happened, as written by Don Kopriva for *Track & Field News:*

"The trouble started with less than a half-mile remaining in the race, at which juncture Cusack had about an eighty-yard lead over Shorter. Cusack then missed a loop in the course and shortened his route by

81

roughly 200 yards. He later claimed that someone had directed him wrong, but Haydon (meet director Ted) subsequently denied that his officials, few and far between though they were, had seen anyone wave the NCAA champ down the wrong path.

"Shorter took the same route as Cusack, although he reportedly realized his mistake and backtracked, costing himself 50 yards in the process. The real villain in this drama, however, is the course itself, which was poorly marked with small flags. A white line laid down earlier to mark the route had been essentially demolished by a spate of rain and snow which had preceded the run."

The AAU, in an attempt to placate the involved parties, arbitrarily placed Cusack fourth, which apparently satisfied no one. Cusack refused to accept his award. Jack Bacheler, Shorter's Florida Track Club teammate, appeared instead of Frank to pick up the gold medal.

8
Around the World

What can one conclude about a culture that sterilizes cross-country running by stretching out on soft, manicured golf courses? In cross-country, too, we are the affluent society. I prefer to think that American runners are cheated, not spoiled, by the dearth of authentic cross-country runs in the United States. It is not that we must make a tough sport even tougher to further distinguish it; it is that we must try at times to meet the world standard, which is one that blends imagination and intensity, making cross-country running an unforgettable experience.

My own running in this regard is limited, having ventured outside the US only to the Canadian Rockies, a wonderful retreat, and to other Canadian running haunts such as Mont Royale Park in Montreal and Stanley Park in Vancouver. So I am going to let my friend, neighbor and occasional running partner—when he is in the States—Jim O'Neill tell you a little about cross-country worldwide.

Jim works in sales promotion for an international banking firm that periodically relocates him and his family in a far-off land. The O'Neills have made numerous trips abroad and casually travel to Europe as I would make an overnighter to Philadelphia. Jim is 40 years old and does not look a day over 30. This is true; I am not patronizing him. He has a boyish face to begin with, and he has sustained his well-being and youthful glow with steady running and an easy-going disposition.

Jim never gets mad. Well, almost never. He gets awfully upset when threatened during a run by dogs and mischievous kids. I recall the day one winter when we had two miles to go on a route I christened as "The O'Neill 10-Miler." (Jim was not satisfied with our up-and-back road route on hilly Staten Island. The European influence was apparent as he devised an intricate course that maximized the use of hills in the immediate vicinity.)

It had snowed heavily the night before, and lurking behind a hastily built snow hut were a few unknowing young boys. They did not consider that when they rifled snowballs at us, one brushing O'Neill, Jim would run up to them and, holding firmly the neck of one, lecture on manners and respect in a civilized society. This unnerved them more than would the retaliatory snowball I assumed O'Neill would plant on their mugs.

I have also christened an act of dog-repellent as "The O'Neill Yell." A few years ago, Jim told me that dogs basically are cowards. He said that a runner could drive back a threatening dog by standing his ground and ranting wantonly. Since then, I have used this method many times (to the amusement of local residents), and it has never failed.

O'Neill was a quarter-miler at Seton Hall University in New Jersey in the early '50s, and spent time in the service and in the newsroom of a weekly newspaper before getting into marketing and, later, into distance running. Most recently, he lived in Frankfurt, West Germany, for two years, then departed for Hong Kong where he is now living. During that brief visit, in March 1977, Jim narrated for me a splendid slide show of his travels. When he got settled in Hong Kong, he wrote me about cross-country running there. This is how he describes it:

Long-distance running is almost a different sport here because of the incredible hills and paths you have to negotiate. To avoid the traffic (it would be suicide to run downtown), the runner is forced into the mountains where there is no lack of quiet trails.

However, there is no such thing as a straight, flat section for anything longer than about 50 yards. Either the course bends and twists around the contours of the mountains on unpaved, rocky roads, or it climbs murderously up and down. There are hills here, which I run every day, that would make Scarsdale (in New York, site of an annual hilly road race) look like a billiard table.

There is one cruel affair called Wanchai Gap Road, which I did not think was runable the first time I saw it. It is a half-mile climb up a grade so steep that your knees are practically hitting your chin at some points. After about five attempts I am now able to reach the top, but when I do my legs are so rubbery with fatigue that it is difficult to continue to run or even walk.

This is bad, because the next part of the course is another hill appropriately called "The Black Slink." This is about two-thirds of a mile of steady uphill, about half the grade of Wanchai Gap, but ever upward, twisting and turning up the contours of Victoria Peak. It is not possible to avoid these hills (or similar ones) if you want to get out of the congestion, fumes and traffic on the flats below.

I ran in a 10¼-mile race over a course that would kill 80% of the starters in a US race. It was won in over 65 minutes by a 2:38 marathoner, so you have some idea of the difficulties. It was the only time I had ever run a course that made me frightened.

It was just plain dangerous! You could literally get killed on the course, as there are numerous downhill sections over rocky and eroded surfaces that are only two or three feet wide, with sheer drops of a few hundred feet. Many runners finished the course with bloody arms and legs from falls suffered during the race.

I did not fall, but I did get lost only about one mile from the finish. Six of us simply went straight where we should have turned left—another hazard of the course.

Cross-country in Hong Kong must be described as survival running, because the first goal is to finish the course—alive. It is no accident that the Gurkha soldiers stationed in Hong Kong monopolized the races. For centuries, they have had a reputation for being the toughest mercenaries in the world. I'm convinced that if a serious cross-country runner (European style) trained for six months on the mountains of Hong Kong, he would not be intimidated by any course in Europe.

O'Neill then summarizes some of what he's seen in Europe:

In Europe cross-country plays an entirely different role in the sporting scene. There, cross-country is a respectable sport in its own right. Major races are covered on television, and I get the impression that many of the runners specialize in this type of running and are not just conditioning themselves.

Courses typically include streams to ford, fallen trees to hurdle, muddy pits to wade through and other delights. I remember watching a meet held in Berlin on TV and seeing the runners practically sliding down and through some mucky sections, emerging finally with that haggard, filthy look of cyclists at your typically muddy motocross.

In Germany, running facilities are superb. One does not run on public roads in Germany, not unless one has a death wish. One runs in a park. Parks there are very neat, safe and sanitized. There are woods surrounding all German cities (the pagan Germans were tree worshippers), and the woods are criss-crossed with two- or three-meter wide paths, all immaculately maintained.

GERMANY

Another colleague of mine who has run cross-country in Germany is Hal Higdon, a world-class Masters runner and author most recently of the book *Fitness after Forty*. In a letter to me, Higdon writes, "I spent a year and a half in Germany in the mid-'50s and the Germans, at least at that time, ran in the forests at rather short distances on nice but undemanding courses—at least the few I ran on, in places like Munich and Stuttgart. I ran 1500-meter and 5000-meter cross-country runs, for instance, and usually they were part of multi-distance events for all ages and sexes, so sometimes you could even double since the events went on all day. But there wasn't anything in the way of a course that severely challenged you, although I am willing to concede that I may have missed the tough ones. I had the impression that what I ran in was somewhat typical of German cross-country."

Further amplification of German cross-country is provided by Lothar Hirsh, the national long-distance coach of the German Athletic Federation. In a five-page letter to me in June 1977, Hirsh outlined the German system from top to bottom. Here are the key elements:

Organized German cross-country was in an undeveloped state until a few years ago when a structure was designed to make national teams more competitive in the International IAAF meet and to better prepare athletes for the track season. Races are conducted on weekends throughout the winter, at a range of distances for men and women of all ages.

There is individual and team scoring—teams meaning clubs. There are also separate championship meets just for students and teenagers. They prefer to run on flat tracts of open land—fields, forests and meadows—but are seeking more challenging terrain in order to acquire a style of course more identifiable with German cross-country.

The German championship, now held two weeks prior to the IAAF run, consists of 15 separate races over two days. The senior entrants, long-distance men, run 11,500 meters. The juniors go 9600 meters and the senior women 5750 meters.

Besides the German championship, there is a meet called the "National Championship." How the latter differs, I could not ascertain, although I am sure that the "German" meet has nothing whatsoever to do with East Germany. I speculate that the second meet mentioned may have a particular club emphasis to it. Furthermore, even though German runners tend to enter 8-12 competitions, training receives priority, for cross-country is still subordinate to the track season.

Quoting Lothar Hirsch: "There are no cross-country specialists in the Federal Republic of (West) Germany. Cross-country running may be considered as being a means to optimize track performance."

BELGIUM

Belgium, on the other hand, has a glorious tradition in cross-country, the direct result of the concerned proprietorship held over it by national authorities. The Belgians take their cross-country very seriously and are proud of the remarkable victory record by Gaston Roelants in the IAAF. In fact, the 1977 champion, Leon Schots, is from Belgium. So is Eddie Declerck, the current chairman of the IAAF's Cross-Country Committee.

Victor Goyens, general secretary of the Royal Belgium Athletic League (founded in 1889), informed me that there are 250 organized cross-country races every season in Belgium, a country with a total land area not much larger than the state of Maryland. He also sent me an extract from a publication entitled *La Vie Athletique* (*The Athletic Life*) which describes in French the Belgium cross-country setup. Applying rusty high school French, I am able to discern certain points.

There are eight age categories for men, from "pupilles" who run 1000 meters up to seniors who run 12,000 meters and to veterans (i.e. Masters) at 8000 meters. Except for the absence of veterans, women have the same divisions, but their competitive limit is 11 races per season. Senior women race 5000 meters; their courses are recommended to be as flat as possible.

The Belgian athletic congress dictates all policy. Many events are club-oriented, and a runner is not authorized to take part unless affiliated with a registered club, which pays the congress 1500 francs (men) or 1000 francs (women) to gain legitimate status. When gifts are awarded as prizes, it is forbidden to announce their value prior to the race. The season begins in November, which is customary in the Northern Hemisphere (except in the US and Canada where it *ends* in November). They run a set of provincial championships, two weeks before the Nationals and a month before the IAAF.

Manfred Steffny, an Olympic marathoner from West Germany, was impressed with a Belgium cross-country race in which he ran in the winter of 1972. He was working for his country's Sports Information Service and told of his experience in the April 1973 issue of *Runner's World*. George Beinhorn translated from German the article excerpted here:

The stands are tightly packed. Thousands will escort the runners around the stadium track, over meadows and fields. The television people point their light meters at the sky and make helpless gestures. It is gloomy. They will only be able to deliver mediocre picture quality. But the Belgians are sitting in front of TV screens as if it were a great bicycle race, quivering with their favorites and happy in their warm barroom, while the ones out there in the mud . . . .

Start! At maximum speed, 150 runners of the main event are off. From the broad line of the stadium field, the course goes after barely 200 meters through a little straw-dressed gate onto the fields. It's cross-country. Woe to him who hasn't threaded the needle with the lead group. His hopes for a good place sink to nil.

The snow is melted; the open runners have left behind a deep rut. We sink in almost to our ankles at every step; the mud tries to suck our feet in tight. No matter, up to now it's going very well. Out of the stadium with the first 30.

Cross-country running separates the wheat from the chaff. In every track run, you can see ambitious runners overestimating themselves, mixing it up with the leaders for the first half. Not in cross-country. To hold on with the leaders for the first 500 meters, a condition and agility are required that only a class runner possesses. Often enough, the order of the first 10 is the same after nine or 12 kilometers as it was at three. Only the gaps have grown.

But we were still in the middle of the first lap. A fence and a stream have been jumped, then there's a gurgling, bubbling marsh where one sinks almost to the knees. It is the hardest kind of work, this stretch. One rows with his arms, struggles and fidgets with his legs. Are my shoes still on, or have they gone down? At last, there is something like a path.

Suddenly, a railroad embankment appears. It's no mistake; the flags indicate it's part of the course. Away it goes, over the railroad ties of a retired line. Three or four ties at a time? Terrible, inhuman, this race!

From the second round on, one looks forward to this section, because there's a trailing wind, and also the filth and water run out of your shoes. Then back to the stadium. Obstacles wound with straw thatching wait for the runners. The team attendants call out no splits. That's senseless here. They count, "26th, 27th, 28th. . . ."

One lap is gone. What, eight more? Impossible! I have already fallen in the mud. Shirt and pants are completely filthy; a crust of mud is stuck fast to the cheek, and in my mouth I still have the sweetest taste of earth that just won't be spit out.

Few quit in these cross-country runs, although the so-called inner swine is harder to overcome than in track runs. Again and again, the will whips the tortured body on. Because one is already feeling so bad that it can't get any worse.

The crowd applauds each runner, but the one who stops is no longer considered to be a marvelous athlete but one of their own. They laugh at his appearance the way they would laugh at a fellow sitter who'd slipped on a banana peel. Suddenly, it's fun.

Yes, it is odd. Man is incredibly adaptable, a creature of habit. War, jail, forced labor, everything can become everyday to him. Just so can he be happy at kilometer six of a cross-country run. The tricks of the ground are more familiar now. Run way over on the left here; jump off at that spot there. Energy is better distributed. A rhythm is discovered. It all becomes just half as bad, no matter if one is overtaken or passes someone else.

Finally, the mud bath is over. We go under the showers in full vestments. The most important utensil is not soap but a knife. You can cut open your running shoes—they can't be removed from their feet any other way—and scrape the mud off arms and legs. And after this preliminary work, the soap has its say. It is a genuine long-distance shower.

BRITAIN

The modern era of cross-country originated in Great Britain and thrived in the late 19th century, and to this day its conduct of the sport is exemplary. In the *Runner's World* booklet, *The Varied World of Cross-Country*, published in 1971, British writer Wilf Richards describes the English setting:

"That the winter sport of cross-country running is immensely popular in England can be deduced by the fact that close to a thousand runners turn out for the senior national championship race alone. And bear in mind that this is a team event in which each club is limited to one team of nine members. Many hundreds of runners who are out with their clubs week after week are excluded from this huge national field. Almost all British distance runners take their cross-country activities just as seriously as their track events.

"The sport is very rarely brought to a halt on account of bad weather. Torrential rain, snow and ice, gale-force winds, freezing temperatures—all these are accepted as part of the game. Courses vary considerably, though they are usually what could be described as 'traditional,' with a few gates or fences to be negotiated, some ditches or streams to cross, some hill climbs, as much grassland and as little road as possible, and, in short, a course with as much variation as can be obtained in these days of diminished countryside. Distances are usually around seven miles, rarely less, while in the area and national championships, the seniors have nine miles to cover."

SPAIN

Author Pat Tarnawsky Warren describes the Spanish scene at "El Cross":

"On the sunny afternoon of Feb. 14, 1971, a scene familiar to all of us took place in a big, wooded city park. As cheerful crowds braved the chill breeze, a whopping total of 5800 boys and girls rampaged over the rolling cross-country course. The eight events ranged from 1500 to 9000 meters. It might have been one of those mass meets so typical of the booming West Coast US cross-country scene.

"But it wasn't. The setting was the Casa del Campo park in Madrid. The meet was the Gran Premio de la Juventud, Spain's biggest age-group cross-country affair. In fact, those 5800 entrants are an awful lot by *any* country's standard—especially when you consider how small Spain is.

"Long-distance running finally has hit Iberia. And hit it hard. In general, Spanish running activities seem concentrated between Madrid and the north Atlantic shore. One reason for this could be temperament. Distance running seems more suited to the energetic northerners than to the Adalusians of the hot south.

"In fact, most of the big races take place on the north shore. Since the Gulf Stream hits that coast, its climate is mild year-round—never above 80 in the summer, never below freezing in the winter, with a lot of rain and mist. This makes for ideal racing conditions, in contrast to the torrid summer heat and bitter winter cold that runners have to face farther south. (Most Americans think of Spain as a land of palms and pleasant sun 365 days a year. Nothing could be further from the truth.)"

MEXICO

Peter Burkhart was a resident of Mexico when he wrote of a mountain race he entered:

"The city of Puebla is in southeastern Mexico, high in the central plateau country of 7000-feet-plus elevation. This is my home amid the towering crags of four volcanoes which stand like sentinels around the 'city of angels.'

"I usually train at a local high school which is more like a beautiful botanical garden with its multi-colored plants, flowers and winding grass pathways. My jogging was about a month along from scratch when I was approached one day by a local sports instructor, Maestro Guerro.

"The maestro came across the grass infield and took a seat beside me.

"'Manana, we go in the bus, yes?'"

"'Where?'

"'Up to Tepozuchiti.'

"The school had received an invite to run, and some of the boys wanted me along. Although my physical condition was far below par, I was enthused with the chance to see the inside of a Mexican military complex.

" 'What type of race is it?'

" 'Cross-country on a hill,' " the maestro replied.

"The whistle for assembly blew at 11 a.m., and the ground seemed to open as the runners poured out of barracks and vehicle sections. The final count was 20 complete teams and 140 starters. I was really shell-shocked to see such a large field. A quick look at the footgear revealed that 90% were decked out in big, heavy basketball sneakers. Now everyone knows that good racers don't wear these, right?

"It was a typical Van Cortlandt Park-type race with a flat-out sprint for the first corner. We went by a series of military buildings and up a hill which was about 300 yards steep. I was sandwiched in a huge group in the vanguard as we hit a level area. I put on a burst to get loose, but so did the others and we roared around another corner as one. My legs wobbled as they beheld another hill with no crest in sight.

"I was soon reduced to a quick walk and had the opportunity to look at the scenery. Although the colors were all blurred, I could make out the city of Puebla below at 7300 feet, and I was still going up. One soldier ahead of me lost his footing and fell. He was lucky indeed, for another foot to the left and he would have been a paratrooper without a chute. It was all I could do to just keep putting one foot in front of the other. This is a cross-country course?

"I went up and over the summit on my last breath. It was a sharp turnaround. Down I started like an express train, disregarding rocks and runners. Along the cliffs I raced with one eye on the rim and the other watching for numerous dropouts. They were in tough shape at this stage of the game. The sun beat down harshly, and my face and neck were like a Vera Cruz lobster. It was brutal!

"I didn't gain any places or lose any on the descent. For all practical purposes, the race was over at the peak. The soldier just ahead of me at the end went all-out to keep this place and collapsed as he crossed the finish line. He was out cold!"

NEW ZEALAND

Jack Foster, still a world-class marathoner at age 45, writes of the cross-country scene in his native New Zealand, where there exists a thriving club system.

"The club which I belong to," says Foster, "has a dozen or so keen seniors (not veterans) including a store manager, teacher, scientist, surveyor, civil engineer, mechanical engineer, clerk, draftsman, two farmers and two plumbers. I would say most of our top men are over 25 years and long out of school, quite the opposite of the US system where the best men are mostly school men or just beyond."

Barry M. Meyers, secretary of the New Zealand Amateur Athletic Association, has written to me about his country's cross-country system. Some significant points:

Cross-country is administered through the Athletic Association, which is mainly a track and field body. The season runs from April to mid-September, and there is a mixture of events, some open only to clubs and others of the all-comer variety. The distances are from 8000-12,000 meters. One season's-end event was given as 20 miles—"actually about half cross-country and half road."

Meyers notes, "Our courses are severe by world standards, often containing a good deal of hill, bog, creek and the like. Most of our harriers like it that way. The great majority of our track stars over the years have also been harriers. Peter Snell, for instance, won a New Zealand cross-country title, as did Rodney Dixon."

Meyers adds, "So far as school events are concerned, this is largely left to the individual schools, some of which have at least an annual cross-country race. Recently, the country's high schools have begun to conduct their own national championship, but this is run entirely by the school and the competitors are not all registered athletes (with the NZ AAA). The total number of harriers in the country would be of the order of 5000-6000, with all three of the largest centers, Auckland, Wellington and Canterbury, having over 1000 each."

AFRICA

Transplanted Africans have excelled in American cross-country. Geoff Fenwick tells how the sport operates in their homeland:

"In a purely informal way, African cross-country tradition is magificent. The largest map reveals relatively few roads there. Yet if you flew over the land you would see that it is criss-crossed with innumerable trackways created by both animals and men. Long experience has made the African skilled at moving over this type of countryside.

"In most areas outside the towns, people travel on foot. And although the nomads of the Sahara depend upon animals for their transport, one must not forget that the toughest and most natural of all men traverse the wastes of the Kalahari Desert on foot. In his own environment, there is little doubt that the Kalahari Bushman would be a match for the world's best cross-country runners.

"Very, very few athletic clubs are open to the general public, partly because most African people live in scattered communities and partly because financing open clubs is difficult in underdeveloped countries. Thus, a high percentage of the population is automatically eliminated, and the responsibility for cross-country running rests with schools, colleges, military and quasi-military organizations. Not that rugged individuals like the Bushmen and the Masai are very 'clubable,' anyway.

"Obviously, climatic factors rule out the hot, damp regions of the west. In the east, where heat is tempered by altitude, cross-country exists in the form of infrequent competition. Not surprisingly, the highlands of Kenya is an important center for the sport. Many of Kenya's best long-distance men, Kip Keino included, have competed in the annual Maseno cross-country race which, if memory serves me right, crosses the Equator during its course.

"One of the successful nations is Ethiopia, although there is not a great amount of competition there. Much training is carried out over rocky countryside, however, and this holds Ethiopian runners in good stead when they compete in cross-country races. They have tackled European races with success, and among their representatives have been such stalwarts as Abebe Bikila and Mamo Wolde.

"Closer to Europe, Morocco, Tunisia and Algeria also produce good cross-country teams. In these countries, there is a definite winter season. There has also been the influence of France. Examine the list of French internationalists as far back as the 1930s, and it will become evident that France depended, to some extent, on her colonies for a supply of talented long-distance runners. El Ouafi and Alain Mimoun, both French winners of Olympic marathons in their time, were North Africans, and there have been others.

"Yet the fact remains that at present cross-country is a needless, artificial sport to the vast majority of people in Africa. Given good health, most Africans are basically fit in any case. As the continent becomes more 'developed,' the people might feel the need for sport as we know it, including cross-country racing—as opposed to cross-country *running* which so many of them already do in leading their daily lives. But by then the most interesting ones, like the Bushmen, may not be with us."

SOUTH AFRICA

Fenwick speaks knowledgeably about most of Africa but neglects to deal with South Africa. I have been in correspondence with a high school coach from Natal named Doug Andersen, who has been helpful in explaining the role of the sport there. Says Andersen:

"Cross-country in South Africa is not regarded as a short, sharp toughening process for the forthcoming track season but is taken as a full-time and separate winter activity. In fact, very few serious track runners bother with cross-country, because the longer-than-average championship distance of 12 kilometers is seldom worth their while. The length of our season is five months, and competitors are mainly cross-country specialists and younger road runners. We do have a Masters section but only one age grouping (i.e., 40).

"South Africa does not have a highly organized college setup as in the USA. There is a national universities championship, but the university teams compete as clubs in the leagues which are an essential part of our cross-country structure. Track and field is not that well supported in S.A., as the national sports of rugby and cricket—rugby especially—are virtually the national religion."

Each of the 13 provinces has a league program of six or seven races, followed by a provincial championship and finally the nationals. The venue for the nationals alternates betweeen high-altitude and sea-level sites. Andersen continues:

"Courses vary from very easy, fast playing-field-style courses, run mainly by the Afrikaan-speaking areas (a Dutch dialect) to the very tough, hilly, often rough underfoot courses run in the English-speaking areas. As a result our best track runners (Bonzet, Malan, Krogman, Van Zijl, etc.) are nearly all Afrikaaners, while our marathon strength lies mainly in the coastal provinces. A multi-racial South African team is selected each season to run against Rhodesia, Lesotho, Malawi and Botswana in Rhodesia."

Andersen claims that ineffective coaching is "our biggest problem. There are very few coaches capable of inspiring much confidence in a national-class athlete. The majority of our athletes coach themselves— their theories being many and various, and based largely on hearsay. As a result, many bright prospects soon fade into obscurity."

Andersen cites one example: "A 15-year-old athlete with plenty of promise was recently congratulated in a club newsletter for his 'display of guts' and his 'fine example' because he was fool enough to run 800 meters, 1500 meters, 5000 meters and the 3000-meter steeplechase all in one afternoon!"

Of the high schools, Andersen discloses, "It is greatly restricted by the emphasis placed on rugby. At most schools, rugby is compulsory, and principals promote the game as one played by 'men.' As a result, we only have all the broken-down stretcher cases to use in our cross-country teams. In 1976, we won the national schools championship."

Andersen works at the Westville Boys High School. Here is how he operates: "My style of coaching assumes that (a) the athlete is lazy, (b) has many distractions such as surfing, scrambling, etc., and (3) is very strictly disciplined—S.A. schools are very strict.

"I've tried to make what is really a difficult sport as attractive as possible by (a) making training voluntary (rugby training is compulsory); (b) team T-shirts; (c) school awards; (d) progress trophies; (e) nationwide tours. All in all, I try to make my athletes feel that they belong to a select group within the school. Success has, of course, helped as the team has lost only twice in six years—the last time being four years ago."

Training at championship-caliber Westville: "My top athletes train twice per day when racing allows, and some reach 100 miles per week. I don't let them hold mileages like this for very long and only allow my under-15 athletes to reach 60 miles per week."

Andersen's wife has the deliciously-sounding name of Felicity, which in English means happiness and good fortune. However, the Andersens had their share of bad luck recently when they embarked on a cross-country mission of extraordinary planning and ambition. Early in 1976, Andersen wrote to me in my capacity as publisher of *The Harrier*. He told me of the success of his team and of his hopes to arrange for his squad a competitive tour of the US during the fall season of 1976. I published his remarks as a letter to the editor. This generated interest among some US high school coaches who contacted Andersen expressing their inclinations to host a visit from his entourage.

His first letter to me was dated March 18, 1976, and he indicated that on his end "everything—accommodations, transport—the lot" had been organized. He was all set to arrive in the US on Dec. 6, 1976, and tour for a month or so. He had contacted 135 schools and had received 35 replies. All he needed were the specific teams to race against. After numerous trans-Atlantic phone calls at a cost to him of $1000, Andersen finally established seven firm race dates with teams from seven different states. He had raised $22,000 through cake sales, raffles and the like.

Frankly, this surprised me. When Andersen first told me of his plans,

I was delighted to oblige him with information but was doubtful that he could pull it off in light of South Africa's precarious position of late on the international sports scene. After the Olympic debacle (to cite the most glaring of many conflicts), I wondered how a white South African team could get a welcome mat laid for it by image-conscious US officials? Unfortunately, my instinctive reaction proved to be partly true.

"The AAU tried to ruin everything," alleges Andersen. "They even sent a telegram to us three days before we left, saying stay home because it will not be possible for us to run against anyone. The National Federation of State High School Athletic Associations sent me several rude letters. They were offended because I had not asked them for permission to run, and try as I might I could not convince them that in S.A. we have never heard of them!

"Eventually, they sent me a letter telling me that they had contacted all the schools that we were going to run against and that all the fixtures had been cancelled. This devastated me, but I phoned one of the coaches to find out the full story, and he didn't even know what I was talking about. Therefore, I quickly phoned all the coaches only to find that none of them knew anything about it. It cost me $300 in phone calls to find out that the Schools Federation was taking a chance and had spun a bullshit story.

"Anyway, we ignored them all and came to the US anyway, and our wonderful hosts soon proved to us that the opinions of the associations are not necessarily those of the athletes."

In all fairness to the National Federation and AAU, both agencies originally greeted the proposed tour with understanding, if not encouragement.

In a March 30, 1976 letter to the AAU's Pacific Association (contacted by Andersen) then-AAU track and field administrator Robert C. Lafferty wrote:

"The Union of South Africa has been suspended by the IAAF. The suspension means that their athletes are not allowed to represent their country, nor be representatives of a national team, nor wear the colors of South Africa. For this reason, we could not send an official letter of invitation.

"If the athletes choose to come to the United States on travel permit conditions, which would indicate that they are duly registered amateur athletes, then we would have no intentions of refusing them the opportunity to compete."

Similarly, in an April 21, 1976, letter to Andersen, Clifford B. Fagan, executive secretary of the National Federation, wrote:

"The cross-country season in the United States is over or practically over during the first week in December. I personally do not know of any secondary schools, that is high schools, that compete after the first week in December. Therefore, I will not be able to assist you in securing competition at that time. We would be very pleased to help you if you could bring your team to the United States during our normal season, that is during September, October or November."

The problem arose when word of the impending tour circulated within the ranks of the AAU and National Federation, and officials discovered that their initial feelers of good will, however well-intentioned, were presumptuous and ignorant—causing them, I would think, some embarrassment. In fact, they were in direct contravention with the International status—or, the *non-status*—of South Africa.

At my request, Ollan C. Cassell, executive director of the AAU, explained the AAU's posture to me in a letter of May 17, 1977. It reads, in part:

"In short, the South African team could not compete in this country, nor any other country that holds membership in the International Amateur Athletics Federation. The IAAF lifted South Africa's membership at the last Olympiad.

"Every effort was made to prevent the trip, as it would constitute a violation of international rules. As such, the AAU could neither condone nor sanction this visit.

"Prior to the South Africans' departure, cables were sent from here to both the Westville Boys High School and the South African AAU advising them of our position.

"No threats were made to anyone; merely statements of fact regarding competition against non-IAAF nations, especially one that has been barred from international competition.

"It is unfortunate that young athletes like the South African cross-country team members should be victims of politics. Rules, however, are rules and must be obeyed, for the greater good of all athletes concerned, especially our own here in the US. Our actions were meant to protect American runners from punitive action by the IAAF."

Richard C. Shafer, Fagan's assistant at the National High School Federation, was also kind enough to answer my inquiry. In a March 21, 1977 letter, he stated:

"Application for sanction of a tour by his team was submitted and approved for California only. Because the tour did not meet standards in other states, it cannot be approved in these areas. Each individual state high school athlete association has certain criteria, as does the National Federation, concerning competition of this nature. When these criteria are satisfied, competition is approved regardless of whether it is interstate or international."

Notice, though, how the letters from Cassell and Shafer contradict one another. If, as Cassell asserts, "The South African team could not compete in this country," how can it be approved, as Shafer contends, "for California only"? Is California still in the Union?

While Andersen was haggling with the AAU and National Federation, the USTFF was most cordial to him—up to a point. Listen to Carl W. Cooper, the USTFF executive director, in an April 13, 1976, note to Andersen:

"This office could probably arrange for you to have special rates at hotels and motels and could probably arrange competition for you in the warmer climates of our country in December. . . . We could work out an itinerary. . . . In the event that you have further interest in such a trip to the US please correspond with me and give me plenty of time in which to arrange matters."

But then on Oct. 12, 1976, Cooper wrote:

"I deeply and sincerely regret to inform you that in no manner can the USTFF be connected with your proposed tour of the US. My Executive Committee has overruled me in connection with your tour, and there is nothing that I can do to change their minds. I deeply regret encouraging you over the phone, but I thought that there would be no problem in the manner of assisting you or having you run under the banner of the USTFF."

So Andersen and his team were rebuked on all possible fronts. He was discouraged but still determined. "We ignored all disapproval (both in SA and USA)," he says flatly.

Andersen adds, "There was no red tape in South Africa. The SA AAU does not control school athletics. Therefore, we can do what we like. The only controlling body that could have stopped us would be the schools' controlling body, and they would never do that because *I'm* the chairman! We didn't have anything to do with the US State Department, because we came on visitors' visas.

"In fact, it is this lack of interest in garbage like red tape that has caused me considerable hassle here. I have been officially reprimanded by the Department of Education for going about the organization without keeping the principal informed. What you Americans don't

98

understand is that South Africans are very narrow and small-thinking in their outlook—very conscious of authority and rank, and anyone ambitious is viewed with jealousy and suspicion. Often, his plans will be vetoed by an older man in a position of authority."

Yet, with all this, the tour was smashing. Here is Andersen's completed itinerary, as sent to me verbatim:

Dec. 3, 1976: Left South Africa.

Dec. 4: Free day in Amsterdam.

Dec. 5: Stayed with friends in Chicago. First experience of snow for many of us. Suffering from nine hours of jet lag.

Dec. 6: Arrived Seattle. Struck by beauty of area, especially Mt. Rainier. Visited Kingdome. Same size as our outdoor stadiums. Banquet and social in our honor. Kids spent day at Hazen High School giving talks on S.A. and answering questions. Race on shores of Lake Washington—freezing cold. Toured U. of Washington campus. Had some beautiful training runs. Especially fascinated by Boeing setup. Unfortunately, unable to visit factory. Kids all made pigs of themselves at Ferrell's ice cream parlor.

Dec. 9: Arrived Portland. Visited Mt. Hood. What a beautiful sight. Toured Multnomah Sports Club. Race in very cold conditions. Most races very hush-hush affairs. Some of the coaches phoned by the AAU and warned not to run. Just ignored it. Pot-luck supper for us and presented with fantastic photo book on Oregon.

Dec. 14: Arrived Grants, N.M. Terrible cold. No race—AAU strong in N.M. Banquet for us. Visited Indian reservation and Sky City (Acoma Indian Sacred Village). At all the schools so far, the kids and I spent many enjoyable hours talking to classes about S.A.

Dec. 12: Arrived Los Angeles. Too big and dirty. Attended Costa Mesa awards banquet. I had to make a speech (this became quite frequent, because we had so much to thank people for), and they all wanted to know about S.A. Visited Disneyland.

Dec. 17: Arrived Oklahoma City. Two degrees below zero on the day of the race. Visited Cowboy Hall of Fame. Once again, party for us. Met many local coaches at party for me.

Dec. 21: Arrived Tucson. Coach Jim Mielke (Pima JC) took us all the way to the Grand Canyon—unreal!—and on the way, we saw Oak Creek Canyon and Phoenix. Visited US missile base. Very impressive. Visited Mexico as well. Just like our slums at home. (We only saw Nogales). Saw a genuine Arizona sunset—cactus and all. Christmas Day at Grand Canyon.

Dec. 26: Arrived Las Vegas. Wonderful hospitality and fascinating city, but only at night. Drab during the day. Meet sponsored by Nevada Podiatric Society. Went up to mountains near there—had wonderful day sledding. Lost a few dollars attempting to gamble, and saw the Strip and

all the incredible hotels there. Some of the kids saw Hoover Dam. . . .
Spent New Year's Day on a crowded plane. Have you ever tried to sleep
on the benches in Atlanta airport? Don't!

Jan. 4, 1977: Arrived Venice, Fla. Went fishing and enjoyed picking up
fossilized sharks' teeth on the beach. Saw the Ringling Brothers Circus.
Very impressive.

Competitively, the South Africans did very well. They ran seven
cross-country races in 28 days against some of the finer teenage runners
in America and were beaten only by two high school all-star units. In
deference to local AAU pressures, the South Africans twice had to run
out of uniform, and one meet was cancelled altogether. Still, it was the
experience of a lifetime for them.

"We were very surprised to notice the difference between Americans
in different places," Andersen remarks. "Completely different in their
outlook, religion and manner. All very pleasant but definitely different—even their accents were completely different. The hospitality
extended us was absolutely fantastic. The Americans are great people,
and I am at a loss to find the words to thank everyone for everything.

"We ran against, mixed with and stayed with several colored
athletes, and never once was there any ill feeling or embarrassment. In
fact, I can say truthfully that we did not encounter one single incident
of criticism or nastiness—and we came into contact with thousands of
people."

9
The International

In England in the winter of 1903, Alfred Shrubb of Great Britain (who called himself "the world's greatest pedestrian,") won the first International cross-country championship. In Dusseldorf, West Germany, in 1977, at the very end of winter, a Belgian named Leon Schots (who claimed that previously "I never had any success") won the annual world title from a field of more reputable runners than he.

During this period of exactly three-quarters of a century, the International has undergone a guarded metamorphosis. Today, it means different things to different people, and in most quarters of the athletic world, it has yet to acquire the sense of urgency that brushes certain other competitive gatherings.

SHRUBB

Shrubb, born in Sussex in 1878, was a legend in his day. He dominated British track and cross-country, held many world records (amateur and professional) and missed Olympic stardom only because the 5000- and 10,000-meter races, which would have been Shrubb's best events, were not introduced until the Games of 1912 in Stockholm.

Shrubb's success was not confined to standard competition. He raced a fire engine, a horse named Patsey and a relay team of five Americans.

The fire engine event was the initial cue to Shrubb's innate strength. And it was a legitimate contest, not a prank by impulsive youths. It is not exactly clear how the event was established or, for that matter, why anyone would desire to race against a fire engine—one on its way to a fire, no less. Shrubb and a small field of other runners took off for the fire, which was blazing 3-4 miles from the starting point.

As J. Murray of England tells it, "Shrubb was first, the engine second and the other runners nowhere."

Some years later, Shrubb challenged Patsey, a trotter, to a 10-mile race on the Riverside Track in Winnipeg, Canada. Shrubb got out-kicked. Patsey pulled away from him in the last quarter-mile to win by 15 yards. Shrubb's time of 52:20 was exceptional even by today's standards but still not his best performance.

Out to atone for this setback, Shrubb, in January of 1908, ran a 10-mile race against a five-man American team composed of men described as "about the best in their district." Naturally, Shrubb was victorious; only one of the Americans could outrun him on his two-mile stint.

So it was this modest English gentleman with a neatly-trimmed handlebar moustache, smallish frame and supposedly awkward running style who helped inaugurate the International cross-country event in 1903.

SCHOTS

Seventy-four years later, Leon Schots was a much more surprising winner. In 1975, he won the Belgium national 1500-meter and 5000-meter titles, and the following year Schots missed the Montreal Olympics because of a hernia operation. But the noted Olympic runners, such as medalist Karel Lismont (marathon), Schots' Belgium countryman, and Carlos Lopes (10,000), a bank clerk from Portugal, could not hold onto Schots. Nor could anyone else in the featured men's senior race as the field of 180 runners from 20 nations looped five times around the 1.5-mile Grafenberg Race Course circuit.

This was a horse track, a pretty one at that, carpeted with shaggy green turf, aproned by thick woods and, in the best tradition of European cross-country, punctuated with challenging sand hazards and log barriers.

Schots, of Flemish origin, finished the race with a smile and with arms raised as though carrying a weighted barbell overhead. This posture was not without its symbolism, for the angular, bony-looking Schots had indeed carried the Belgium team to the championship by a scant three points over Britain, where lay the roots of this festival.

BACKGROUND

In its early years, the International was held in England, Scotland, Ireland, Wales, France and Belgium. The British won the first 19 trophies, were stopped by France in 1922 and again in '23, '26 and '27. Shrubb's record of double-victories—he won in 1904 as well as in 1903—was surpassed by the Frenchman Jean Bovier, winner in 1911, '12 and '13.

The affair was run under the auspices of the International Cross-Country Union, an organization comprised mainly of Western European countries. The competition, called the "Cross Des Nations," was limited to member nations, and what resulted was hardly a true worldwide event.

Non-member nations such as the United States and New Zealand were invited to the meet only as "guests" and were not permitted to score. In 1967, a women's race was established but held separately from the men's event. Thankfully, in 1973, the scope of the International was altered for the better when the International Amateur Athletic Federation (IAAF), the world's ruling body on matters of track and field and allied events, took over the reins.

"It was felt by the IAAF that not only should all 152 members of the IAAF have the right to take part," writes John B. Holt, IAAF General Secretary, in a letter to me, "but that also the women's race should be organized in conjunction with the men's senior and junior races every year."

The IAAF still retreated a bit and sat on its semantic backside by first calling the race a "Team Competition," finally adding the word "Championship" to its title in 1976.

Consequently, in the years to come, one expects that the period from 1973 and thereafter will be come to be known as the modern era of the International.

In order to forecast the future of IAAF competitions, it is worthwhile to examine the entry list for the five events, 1973-77, that it has thus far managed. Despite the more authoritative stance that the meet has acquired, the level of participation has gone largely unchanged. Here are the figures, in terms of teams entered:

IAAF CROSS-COUNTRY CHAMPIONSHIP, 1973-1977				
Year	Site	Men's Senior	Men's Junior	Women's
1973	Belgium	18 teams	12 teams	12 teams
1974	Italy	15	13	12
1975	Morocco	24	11	13
1976	Wales	19	15	12
1977	W. Germany	21	15	17

There has been only a slight rise in participation. The boldest increase is with the women, from '76 to '77, owing perhaps to their advancing athletic inclinations, and with the senior men, from '74 to '75, because of the African site within close proximity of many "Third World" nations. In fact, the 1975 race included nine teams from the Middle East and Africa, including the host Moroccans, together with Tunisia the only groups from the bunch to have competed in the previous two IAAF races. Six of the nine withdrew when the races returned to Western Europe in '76 and '77. Only Morocco, Tunisia and Algeria, a surprising eighth in '75, continued to compete.

Western Europe will continue to host the International, at least through 1981. The upcoming schedule: 1978—Scotland; 1979—Ireland; 1980—France; 1981—Spain.

"It is always difficult to choose a suitable cross-country course," claims the IAAF's John Holt, "as certain countries, (e.g. England and Scotland, Wales and the USA) favor heavier, more arduous courses, whereas France, Spain, Belgium and Sweden, for example, prefer flatter courses. Also, the needs of spectators and television have to be catered to—this being the reason why in recent years the races are often held on a (horse-) race course." Holt reports that the 1978 site, Bellahouston Park in Glasgow, provides "a much tougher type of course, being more undulating than the race courses have hitherto provided."

THE US ROLE

Mention of the USA as a possible site for the meet brings a smile to one's face for two reasons. One is political, the other cultural. Of the 11 members of the IAAF Cross-Country Committee, which chooses meet sites, only one (Aldo Scandurra of New York) is an American, while nine are from Europe, and one is from New Zealand. How anxious will the foreigners be to give up their home-course advantages and moderate travel expenses for a costly American trip?

The only reasonable hope for an American International would be the unlikely passage of an IAAF rule that would formally rotate the meet to specified sections of the globe on a sort of round-robin basis.

This brings me to the cultural consideration. Even if the races were to land in the US, could we be assured that the flock of world-class runners would receive the attention it deserves? Would there be thousands of cheering spectators, ample newspaper and TV coverage? For the Little League World Series, yes. For the International cross-country championships, probably not. Consider the embarrassment.

In March, when the races are scheduled, America's influential sports writers are usually soaking in the Florida sun, revealing the wit and wisdom of rookie pitchers in spring training. One could depend on attention from TV's "Wide World of Sports," but the hour-plus time consumed by the International's three races would most likely be condensed into five minutes of capsule coverage sandwiched between cliff diving and motorcycle jumps.

With the IAAF in charge, the International is now quite standardized. The meet is conducted in March (the 25th for the '78 meet) as a climax to the winter cross-country season of most of the IAAF members. (The Americans, meanwhile, are concluding their indoor season.) Teams, not individuals, may take part. The senior men must run at least six and not more than nine runners. Six men score. The distance is generally about 12,000 meters.

The junior men must be under 20 years old on the Dec. 31 of the year of the race. Junior teams must run at least four and not more than six men. Four runners score. Their distance is usually between 7000 and 8000 meters.

The women also have a 4/6 entry rule and score four runners. Their distance varies between 4000 and 5000 meters.

The IAAF guidelines further stipulate the following: "The race shall be run over a course confined, as far as possible, to open country, heathland, commons and grassland. A limited amount of ploughed land may be included. Very high obstacles should be avoided. So should deep ditches, thick undergrowth and, in general, any obstacle which would constitute a difficulty beyond the aim of the competition."

The US role in the International has been a peculiar one. In 1973, it sent only a women's team. In 1974, it sent a women's team and a men's junior unit. Finally, in 1975, a squad of senior men accompanied the others and, lo and behold, the US compiled the best three-race record of any nation—two victories and one fourth (seniors). All three teams also made the '76 and '77 trips.

The vacancies in 1973 and '74 were caused simply by a lack of funds.

Let me rephrase that: not a lack of funds, a lack of *allocated* funds. In 1974, the AAU, after spending its cash in one place or another, decided that there was only enough money left to send one team, not three.

Prodded by Long-Distance Chairman Bob De Celle's anxious lobbying, the AAU decided it would at least finance the junior trip. The seniors would stay home. The women who qualified could go only if they agreed to pay a portion of their expenses. And they did, except for Francie Larrieu, the leading lady.

"I want to go badly," she said. "I'm number one and I'm in great shape. I should run. But it just isn't right. Why should I have to pay $180 in air fare when I'm a member of a United States team? It's ridiculous. Somebody has to stand up and protest."

Although the AAU's commitment is now firmer, it is still not entirely secure. Its policy for the junior team has been to pay only for the first four qualifiers, the number of finishers required for a full team to score in the race. The fifth and sixth qualifiers must foot their own bills, so to speak.

The AAU may be inconsiderate, but not dumb. If, for example, the sixth qualifying junior rejected this policy and thus his berth on the US team, the AAU could depend on the seventh or eighth—somebody along the line—to leap at the opportunity and come forth with the funds. Moreover, even if one of the weaker runners was moved into a scoring slot to compensate in the International for the sudden dropout of a key man, the talented US teenagers would still prevail and win the title. (At this writing, the AAU reportedly obtained additional funding from the private sector that would eliminate this hedging.)

In 1977, however, the AAU almost outsmarted itself. It was fortunate that Chris Fox, a Martinsburg, W. Va., High School senior, the sixth and final qualifier, was able to finance his trip to Dusseldorf. Martinsburg (population 18,000) raised the funds for Fox, who placed 18th in the race and was the final US scorer. He displaced Hal Schultz and Jeff Creer, who beat Fox in the trials but finished 33rd and 34th in Dusseldorf. The US beat Spain by four points. Hail to the Fox!

The US qualifying system for the International is hardly ideal. In 1975, when the AAU's pocketbook was ostensibly vacant, the women were again not even scheduled to make the excursion to Rabat, Morocco. They were saved from obscurity by Chuck Debus, then UCLA women's track coach. Apparently with the AAU's approval, Debus put together an 11th-hour setup in which the women would compete on a "postal" basis at three separate sites. (I can still hear the Europeans laughing.)

In postal competition, athletes run the same distances under the same conditions (usually) at different places, and then the performances are rated comparatively. So, in Phoenix, Ariz., Lamoni, Iowa, and Hiram, Ohio, a woman who could fork up a $100 entry fee could run a 2.5-mile track race—10 laps around a 440-yard oval. Debus' ingenuity and hard work camouflaged the ludicrous AAU policy.

The six women who qualified got their $100 worth. They won the International!

In 1976 and 1977, the arrangement was revised, and the women qualified on the basis of performances in the annual Women's AAU Championship run, in late November. The men's squads do not flow out of the fall cross-country season but rather out of separate races held in the winter. Because of the weather then, these races must be held in the South or on the West Coast where the climate is moderate. The events are somewhat inaccessible to runners from the Northeast, not to mention the clashes that result with the hectic US indoor season.

The entries are thus incomplete in terms of available talent, more so for the senior division. The AAU wisely sought to reduce the absentee-ism and boost its team by declaring in 1976 that the first two American citizens to finish in each of the NCAA and AAU fall cross-country championships would automatically gain berths on the US squad. The remaining positions would still be determined in a separate qualifying trial.

Ric Rojas and Terry Cotton (from the AAU), and Craig Virgin and Herb Lindsay (from the NCAA) were the qualifiers. But only Rojas, a post-collegian, agreed to make the trip. The others were entered in the NCAA Indoor track meet in Detroit on the very weekend the US contingent departed for Dusseldorf. And before, when the trials had come around in February, such luminaries as Frank Shorter and Bill Rodgers did not show up. It's no wonder that the US team placed 12th, its worst showing in IAAF competition.

The junior race also goes off in the middle of winter and in one of America's geographical corners. The entry is comprised of high school runners and college freshmen. Because of the timing and travel restrictions, a few leading contenders usually pass up the race. But our teenage talent is so deep that it easily absorbs these losses.

RECENT RACES

All of this was of no concern to Leon Schots, who outran 180 runners through 12,300 meters of Dusseldorf terrain. He left Portugal's Carlos

Lopes, the defending champion, 40 yards behind in second place and coaxed a time of 37:43 for the challenging route. Kenny Moore, the 1972 US Olympic marathoner (fourth place in Munich) and skillful *Sports Illustrated* writer, aptly characterized the race.

Wrote Moore: "The senior men's race was a shifting spectacle of weariness. This may be the hardest race in the world to win, pitting as it does the best runners from a variety of events: milers against marathoners, steeplechasers against 10,000-meter men. In no other kind of running is the strain so great. The toll of constantly hauling oneself out of sand, over logs and away from surrender is eventually a certain blindness of will. The closest thing to it on the track is the steeplechase. But the cross-country world championship is four times as long."

Besides Lopes, two of the three other IAAF victors were in the field. Erik de Beck of Belgium, who prevailed in 1974, placed 18th. Pekka Paivarinta of Finland, the 1973 champion, finished 83rd. Jeff Wells, a student at the Dallas Theological Seminary (after his graduation from Rice), placed 24th and was the leading American. Mike Bordell of the Air Force, who won the US trial, was 79th. AAU titlist Rojas was 111th.

Belgium's three-point victory over England prompted the IAAF to issue this self-praise: "The victory and the nature of the race confirmed more than anything else the validity of the Cross-Country Committee's decision to maintain the IAAF cross-country championship as a *team* event. The fact that (Eddy) Van Mullem (Belgium), by finishing 51st out of 163 finishing runners assured the team prize for his country; the knowledge that if (Mike) McLeod (the sixth English finisher, in 43rd place), had finished a mere two seconds earlier in 35th place, then England would have won by five points—all this adds incentive for the athlete and a fascination for the team follower."

England and Belgium have sustained a compelling rivalry in the men's division. In 1973, the host Belgians won with England fifth. In 1974, Belgium defeated the English by six points while third-place France was more than 100 points behind. New Zealand, with soon-to-be mile record-holder John Walker in fourth, won the 1975 event, and England edged Belgium for second. In 1976, it was England first, Belgium second and France a distant third.

Back in Dusseldorf, the US juniors extended their streaks in both the team and individual fronts, before a boisterous crowd of 12,000, the likes of which is quite uncustomary in America. The US beat Spain for the second straight year and added to its previous triumphs over Morocco and Ireland. Thom Hunt, a University of Arizona freshman, comfortably won the 7500-meter race from a field of 80 finishers. Hunt was second to his former California high school rival Eric Hulst the year before. Americans also captured the '74 (Richard Kimball) and '75 (Bobby Thomas) events. All four winners are native Californians.

The US women had second place to themselves behind a vastly superior Soviet unit. Spain's Carmen Valero Omedes won her second consecutive title. America was led by Sue Kinsey, a surprising eighth and less than 100 yards out of third. Her teammate, the versatile Julie Brown, was 14th, unable to repeat her 1975 win over Valero when the US captured the team trophy.

Trophies aside, the International has had for the runners, especially the passionate Europeans, a social appeal. England's Dave Bedford, who in 1977 lost his 10,000-meter world record in track to Kenya's Samson Kimombwa, chatted with Kenny Moore the night before the Dusseldorf races.

"You know," Bedford told Moore, "all you do on these trips is talk about past trips. Remember 1970 in Vichy? England won, naturally. We won every year from 1964 to 1972. But the celebration was the thing."

Moore disclosed that "Vichy's revelries included sending a borrowed Peugeot over a bridge into the river Allier."

Bedford's assessment: "Lovely evening that was. . . . It is always a week of seeing old enemies, a hard run and the year's best bash after."

Bedford finished 45th in Dusseldorf. After two miles, he felt a cramp in his foot, tossed away his shoes and completed the course barefoot. Dave's setback came six years after his smashing triumph in San Sebastian, Spain. He won by 22 seconds, a few weeks after capturing the British Nationals by 40 seconds. Incredible!

Bedford trained 200 miles per week, which may have been responsible for the injuries that blemished his career.

HERITAGE AND ROELANTS

While Bedford's 1971 triumph may be the single most impressive in the recent history of the International, the longevity crowns belong to Doris Brown Heritage of the United States and Gaston Roelants of Belgium.

The women's division began in 1967. Heritage won that race—and the four succeeding ones. In 1972, the title went to 35-year-old Joyce Smith, a London housewife and mother, when Heritage did not run. The US-Russian indoor dual meet was scheduled for the same weekend in Richmond, Va., and Heritage competed there.

"I was very upset," she said, "that I had to make a choice. With the Olympics coming up, I need that kind of (track) competition more. But it was still kind of a bad situation. All winter I'd been preparing for cross-country, not track."

Doris returned in 1973 and ran 15th. She was 17th in both 1975 and '76. In 1977, at age 34, she placed 48th. One expects her to compete in 1978 and possibly into the 1980s. Heritage also captured a succession of American titles in track and cross-country. She was a pioneer in women's distance running, often logging 100 miles a week at a time when women were discouraged from even trying the longer events. Her intensity was so compelling that she remarked some years ago, "I was training hard one day and limping the next."

Roelants, the indefatigable Belgium, is perhaps the quintessential cross-country runner. Bearded, with longish, flowing hair, his face shows lines of wisdom and experience. He looks the adventurer, the cautious but self-assured explorer. One expects to find him appearing in a late-night movie cresting a mountain ledge, imploring a rash companion to wait for the storm to break before ascending the peak. But Hollywood, he's not. Roelants knows his mission and he reaches it without fanfare.

Roelants' work in the International spans 13 years. In 1976 at age 39, he placed 13th. He has won four times—in '63, '67, '69 and '72. He was runnerup in '68 and '70. From '73 to '75, he placed eighth, 14th and 10th, respectively. During this period, Gaston also was one of the world's great track steeplechasers, setting the world record and gaining the Olympic title in 1964.

Even at his last cross-country triumph, Roelants, at 35, was an elder statesman rebuking the challenges of young aspirants. The race was back in Britain for the fourth time since 1960, and it was televised live. ("Can the sport have made it at last?" asked one British writer rhetorically.)

Early in the 12,000-meter race, Roelants lost a shoe after an opponent had stepped on it. He stopped, retrieved it and put it back on. He resumed the race and beat Spain's four-time runnerup, Mariano Haro, by more than 100 yards.

Then, at 38, Roelants was 10th in Morocco—a remarkable feat since the 1975 race was the International's most dynamic, not only because of the colorful presence of Third World nations but because of the distinguished field as well. Champions of every ilk merged into this classic footrace of 12,000 meters, held inside the Souissi Hippodrome, a major horse track on the outskirts of Rabat.

The entry list included three Olympic champions: Roelants (steeplechase), Mohamed Gammoudi of Tunisia (5000) and Frank Shorter (marathon); two who would win Olympic titles the following year (New Zealand's John Walker, 1500, and East Germany's Waldemar Cierpinski, marathon); three previous IAAF cross-country winners (Roelants, de Beck, Paivarinta); perennial runnerup Haro; world 5000-meter record-holder Emiel Puttemans of Belgium; European and Commonwealth Games champion Ian Stewart (England), and America's Bill Rodgers, who was to capture the Boston Marathon one month later. It was a Who's Who of Distance Running. Further testimony to its greatness was that New Zealand's Dick Quax, who broke Puttemans' 5000 mark in 1977, placed 91st.

As expected, Walker set a fast pace, one so fast that only Haro, Stewart and Rodgers, not known for his "short" speed, could handle it. Halfway into the race, Rodgers forced the tempo. With 1000 meters left, Haro and Stewart dropped Rodgers from the trio. Stewart later outlegged Haro to the finish. Rodgers was third. Walker faded to fourth.

Tucked away in 15th and 20th positions, far off the pace, were Cierpinski and Shorter, separated by 60 yards. Who would have surmised that on the last day of July in the following year the same 60 yards would separate them on the rainy streets of Montreal with a few miles to go in the Olympic marathon?

Part Three:
METHODS

10
Training

Every fall, when I cover cross-country meets, I have reason to interview the winners and near-winners of dozens of races. I must be at the finish line when they arrive there. I trail them as they warm down and, when I think they are relaxed enough to talk, I approach them, introduce myself and ask them about the race.

There are many standard questions that form the crux of most of these interviews, and the answers to them will be clearly noted in the written account of the meet. When did you take the lead? How did you manage Ballbuster Hill? Was the course rough? Did you realize so-and-so was right on your tail? Will you get the record next week? Height? Weight? Age? Training?

Training! If a physiologist were to study the answers I receive to my probes into the preparation of successful cross-country runners, he would be dumbfounded. To paraphrase: I'm running 90 miles a week and hope to hit 100. . . . Never go over 40 a week. . . . All long, 15-mile workouts at an easy pace. . . . Fast, repeated intervals on the track. . . . Never touch the track during cross-country. . . . We go out on the roads. . . . Hills, hills, hills—that's it. . . . No, no hills—all flats. . . . I

114

ran all summer. . . . Took the summer off. . . . Strict diet—no junk. . . .
Ate pizza and partied last night. . . .

A more specific recollection. On Oct. 1, 1967, my story in *The New York Times* started off:

"Julio Piazza of Brooklyn Tech, who runs 80 miles a week and would like to move up to 100, took the opening scholastic cross-country race of the season yesterday at Van Cortlandt Park, the Bronx. His time was 13:10.4. . . . Officials called it the fastest time ever run over the hilly, 2.5-mile course so early in the campaign."

Two weeks later, on Oct. 15, I wrote in the *Long Island Press:*

"Julio Piazza of Brooklyn Tech has been running less and enjoying it more. . . has reduced his 80-mile-per-week practice load to 60 miles in order to lend more concentration to speedwork. . . . The results were obvious as Piazza lowered his personal best by almost 20 seconds to win the St. John's University Interscholastic run in 12:37.6." (That was a New York City public schools league record and it stood until 1977.)

Of course, we know a good deal more about training today than we did 10 years ago. Yet the Piazza paradox still cries out from locker rooms across the country and the world. Long or short? Fast or slow? Hard or soft? Up or down? Perhaps, as in other medically connected fields, the more we study and test, the more we will realize we do not know. We are dealing with enormous complexities of the human body and mind, and it is no small task to determing how they will react to cross-country running.

In the 1970s, after the political strife of the '60s dissipated, the public became more interested in physical improvement, one by one and family by family, than in solving the collective problems of the nation. The jogging fad became The Jogging Boom. We became preoccupied with our health, we learned of self-awareness and self-help. Get off your butt and live! Be a participant, not just a spectator.

This phenomenon spawned a voluminous outpouring of literature about health and fitness, much of it related in some way to running. We are in the Aerobics Era. . . Speed. Form. Style. Nutrition. Motivation. Philosophy. Equipment. Calisthenics. Everything from repelling junk food to junkyard dogs. While we were once in the dark with such matters, much light has since been shed, and even though some of the widely held theories are inconclusive, enough solid evidence is around to give runners confidence in their efforts.

Training for cross-country is not that much different from training for road running or general distance running. There are the same

115

concerns about conditioning the body and being fit; of striving for and realizing goals; of preparing for possible competition; of improving overall health and well-being; of making it a rewarding and successful experience.

The main factor that separates cross-country from other forms of running is, of course, the terrain to be tackled. There is also the team-oriented structure of the US system and its attendant emphases. The intention of this chapter is to provide a brief, but broad, overview of the latest cross-country training methods. I touch upon many—but not all—bases, for to be thorough would require a complete text in itself.

First, what is your stake in cross-country? Are you a sometimes jogger, following doctor's orders, out to lessen your "punishment"? Are you a year-around road runner out to meet the challenges of a few cross-country races? Are you a fierce competitor from the high schools or colleges out to "peak" for the championships? Are you just getting in shape for the ensuing track seasons? Are you just starting your advancement in running, unconcerned with competition but seeking the diverse high of training off the beaten track? Or are you using cross-country to condition yourself for other sports, such as skiing, swimming, gymnastics or race walking? These are the most populated categories of cross-country runners, or of potential ones. I have their distinct interests in mind for this discussion.

Seventy-five years ago, England's Alfred Shrubb was breaking a number of world records, many of which stood for decades until the great Paavo Nurmi trampled them. In Shrubb's book about cross-country, he told of his appreciation of the sport:

"Of all forms of pedestrianism—and, indeed, of all branches of athletics—there can be nothing superior to cross-country running for either pleasure or health. The sport itself is ideal, whether a race be contested in fine or muddy weather. Track or road running is apt to grow monotonous, however exciting it may be; but there is nothing monotonous in an open country run....Even the training itself is almost as enjoyable as the race, and from the first to last I defy anybody to find a single point to cavil at.

"The varying nature of the ground covered, moreover, assists enormously in building up one's physique and in bringing into play every individual group of muscles, so that the long-distance track runner will be well-advised to devote a fair portion of his attention to field races, as they will materially assist his progress."

Shrubb was well ahead of his time, in both athletic performance and athletic wisdom.

116

OTHER MOTIVES

The muscle tone and overall strength to which Shrubb alluded is wisely sought by athletes who excel in different endeavors. In Alaska, there are high school youngsters who use fall cross-country to prepare for cross-country skiing. In New England, many harriers take to the downhill ski trails after the season.

Eileen Smith, a world-class race walker, ran cross-country for her Long Island, N.Y., high school in 1976.

Curt Alitz of Army, the IC4A champion in 1976, competed successfully on the West Point swim team for two winters instead of running indoor track. He followed the same process in high school and won the national junior pentathlon title. (Cross-country is one of the five events that make up the modern pentathlon.)

One of the most difficult events in track is the intermediate hurdles. Both the 1968 and '72 Olympic intermediate hurdles champions, John Akii-Bua of Uganda and Dave Hemery of Great Britain, had experience in cross-country.

A teenage gymnast who lives not far from me on Staten Island ran on the high school boys' cross-country team before the school established a girls' squad. Her reason: "I always liked to run," said Lisa Perella, a specialist in the horse and uneven bars. "It's good for you. I feel so much better when I'm running, and it relieves my tension. Because I run, I'll have more spring to the horse and more strength in my leg muscles."

These are examples of athletes with both long-term and short-term investments. They wish to develop conditioning for tests that are many months away, yet they need the competitive sharpness for high-powered cross-country races. They are part of a school program and season, and address themselves to a specific type of training I will get to shortly.

Similarly, there are athletes who engage in winter and spring sports—skiing, swimming, hockey, whatever—who have no competitive desires for running. They are well advised to help condition their bodies with ample doses of cross-country training. For them, cross-country may be most important because, unlike purebred runners, the swimmer or skier may not really enjoy running at all. Running around the track or through noisy streets may be the ultimate purgatory for him. Consequently, like the best-selling author James Michener, he needs extra stimuli to get past a workout.

Michener, in his latest book, *Sports in America*, calls jogging "sheer hell," and "one of the world's dullest pastimes." He counters, knowing

117

its physical benefits, "where tennis is unobtainable, I jog. I curse as I do so, but I jog."

Michener would do well to venture out into the woods. His worldwide travels take him to exotic places, to running environments most of us can only dream of. What a marvelous opportunity to get more out of jogging, and of life. If he doesn't believe me, he can ask Kenny Moore, who writes in *Sportsource:*

"The longer one runs, in terms of miles or years, the more one savors cross-country, to feel part of it. A morning run through an agricultural area, even if the same route is repeated for a year, evokes increasing involvement. Patterns of frost and fog, the growth and withering of grass, occasionally cataclysmic events such as lambing, induce an awareness of the land's rhythms—the nearness of his own rhythms, of breath and heart and footfall—assure the runner of his place."

For the James Micheners and for our skiers and swimmers, there should be no training per se, in terms of an organized program. The athletes need to build endurance, and the Micheners crave to sweat and not hate it so much. They are advised to be curious and instinctive, to find interesting places to whet their running appetites and to let their bodies be their gauges. They should make few demands of themselves, other than the exhilaration required to get them back on cross-country earth the following day. The bona fide athlete may require more stress than the overweight pinocle player out to shed 20 pounds before the bathing suit weather of summer.

Thus, we consult an expert. According to Dr. Ernst van Aaken, the noted German coach, endurance-type running brings about, among other things, increased heart volume. Dr. van Aaken prescribes cross-country running for anyone and encourages participants to "run daily, run slowly, with creative walking breaks...run many miles...bring your weight down 10-20% under the so-called norm...consider that breathing is more important than eating and that continuous breathlessness in training exhausts you and destroys your nerves." (The last point is made in repudiation of the interval method, which calls for fast, repeated short runs, often leaving the tired runner considerably out of breath.)

Before leaving these somewhat uninitiated runners out in the forest without a compass, a few hints are in order. Know your route so you won't go astray and be forced to run much farther than you should. Go very slowly on downhill stretches, for concealed bumps can be most unsettling and downright dangerous. Maintain a short stride to facilitate incline ascents and detect abrupt depressions on the flatter

118

surfaces. Use the terrain to your advantage in shielding yourself from high winds, heavy rain or a blistering sun. Do not flirt with very steep hills. Observe less about your body than about your environment; your body will give you automatic signals, but the surroundings are less generous. And one further cautionary appeal: The switch from resilient cross-country terrain to the world on concrete is not taken lightly by feet and legs. Make it a gradual transition.

CROSS-COUNTRY FOR SPRINTERS

These runners have allies in organized track and field. Many of the sprinters and hurdlers in America have virtually no outlet for fall competition. They want to be ready to dash from the starting blocks when the indoor season begins in December or January.

Running the 60-yard dash does not in itself require the stamina of a marathon man. But indoor sprinters are on call for much more. First of all, the 60 may have two or three qualifying rounds run in rapid succession prior to the final. Some sprinters also hurdle. Many of them also run several events—even in one day—up to and including the hard-nosed 600. A foundation of cross-country will help put the sprinter a step ahead of his opposition at the indoor palaces—where only one step can separate first place from last in a jetlike dash.

"Yes," writes Eastern Michigan University Cross-Country Coach Bob Parks, in *The Harrier*, "I believe running cross-country would be beneficial to most sprinters and hurdlers. It provides an excellent base of conditioning...which should prove invaluable when the actual track season begins....Our fall track group warms up each day with a two-mile run around the cross-country course and then goes through a calisthenic-windsprint-jogging-weight training type program....This is a welcome addition to the sprinter's program but not a substitute for proper sprint training."

Parks went on to mention two of his best athletes, Bill Tipton, a hurdler, and Stan Vinson, a quarter-miler. Both ran cross-country in high school and in fall training on the EMU cross-country course, and both have won national honors in track.

Some sprinters become so adept at cross-country that it is difficult to tell they are sprinters. Julio Meade of New York's Andrew Jackson High was one of the nation's finest scholastic quarter-milers in 1966. The previous fall, he was one of the city's top harriers. Also, in November 1971, the lead of a story of mine in the *Long Island Press* read:

"An accomplished sprinter was a hero among distance runners yesterday as Boys High edged Brooklyn Tech for the team title in a

PSAL Cross-Country Championships at Van Cortlandt Park.

"Royd Lake, a 15-year-old junior who ran a 49.1 440 last July, was the key fifth scorer for Boys...."

Getting back to Akii-Bua, the graceful African was reported to have run several cross-country races and placed rather well a short time prior to the 1972 Games. You may recall his Olympic preparation exposed on national television. He was shown running in spurts up a steep hill— more like a mountain—with 25-pound weights on his torso just to keep him honest.

ROAD TO COUNTRY

Serious road runners well beyond their school years, of which in the US there are hundreds of thousands, can slide in and out of cross-country training with ease. Since we are now speaking about experienced runners, they need no special introduction to, or preparation for, cross-country. What they should not overlook or take for granted is the balance that comes into play between their running on the roads and their cross-country divergence.

Road runners sometimes avoid hills, either because they fear them or they are unavailable. Cross-country is a good excuse for slipping in some hill running, if only for variation. (Whether hill running makes you a better runner will be discussed later in this chapter.) One's body, especially the legs and feet, takes an awful beating on the roads, and the cushion-like cross-country turf will be the pause that refreshes. No matter how great your love of the roads, the muck and grime of traffic and congestion are worth bypassing from time to time.

Cross-country also facilitates inflections in the daily workout. On the roads, our freedoms are limited and we have to be on guard for the unexpected. The unexpected does not vanish on cross-country ground, but it is easier there to back away from the excessively regimented schedule into which we sometimes get locked.

Out of the roads, we have our carefully-plotted five- or 10-mile route. We adhere to our arbitrarily imposed boundaries. In the domain of cross-country, we can forget all about that and just run. Run for an hour, two hours, run slowly or at a stepped-up pace, but without that caged-in feeling of "must-do" this or that.

Cross-country can also serve as that rare opportunity to do speed work or tempo work. Most road runners run at roughly the same pace in most of their workouts. This "average" pace is probably between six and eight minutes per mile. They never see a 440-yard track, because the hard intervals the champions do are monotonous, unenjoyable and

120

perhaps invitations to injury.

In cross-country, the interval syndrome can be shaped into different forms for the same benefits. Fartlek, the Swedish term meaning sporadic change of pace, is a natural. Whenever I find myself at a sprawling park, I avoid the traffic route that encloses it and do fartlek workout. It is also important for road runners bent on cross-country racing to become once again accustomed to the nuances of cross-country terrain. The feel of the landscape will improve one's racing judgment.

SCHOOL TEAM TRAINING

This brings us to the school-affiliated runner, specifically the high school and college harrier who dwells in a very tight season. This runner starts his campaign in early September, when the fall semester opens, and culminates it in November with the championship events. This period lasts about eight weeks, and afterwards cross-country usually is cast aside until the next year. New demands follow during the track season.

Because of this structure, most school teams consider cross-country training as a three-step process. Stage One is pre-season, or summer, foundation work. Stage Two is early-season development. Stage Three is peak-season sharpening. I have used the terms "foundation," "development" and "sharpening," because those are the primary functions of the training stages. How are those aims achieved? First, a consensus.

Most distance runners end their spring track seasons in late May or early June, a bit later for the top-level runners who qualify for post-season invitationals or even travel abroad for the European season. After a long year of training, travel and competition, they opt for a break of a few weeks or a month—a physical and mental reprieve. Then, they go into a low-key summer program of daily running at a moderate tempo so that they are sufficiently fit at school's start to join their teammates and go into the next phase of training.

Early in the season the miles are piled on, sometimes at the rate of 100 a week, on cross-country terrain.

Strength and discipline and aggressiveness are the keynotes. Athletes "run through" races, meaning they do not moderate training and rest for them but continue their high-mileage workouts in spite of them.

Then, in anticipation of the conference and national meets, teams reduce mileage but increase pace, and many times venture into interval or fartlek or tempo work to increase their capacities to race at high speeds over long distances. They wish to reach peak condition—the best shape possible for the task at hand—for a stretch of two weeks' worth of the season's most important meets. Peak condition, that elusive running pinnacle, is said to tread a thin line between optimal fitness and physical breakdown. You only know it when you get there.

The running triad I have described is used in one form or another by a majority of the nation's high schools and colleges. There are variations, to be sure, and even utter refutations of this three-step system. Let us look at the specific methods used by many of our finest runners and teams. *The Harrier* magazine conducts an annual high school training survey in which leading runners reveal the composition of their cross-country training. Here are some samples from 1976:

Russell Bowles, St. Christopher's High School, Richmond, Va.
Summer: 1100 miles easy, twice a day running, occasional road racing; 3-4 miles in morning, 8-12 later.
Early-season: Work in a little pace running (slowly); 3 miles in morning, 3 at pace in P.M. with 4 warmup and 4 warmdown.
Peak: Decrease distance slightly, "short and sweet" pace work on hills; 3-4 miles in morning; 4 warmup, 2-3 pacing, 4 warmdown.

Kevin Byrne, Paramus Catholic High School, Paramus, N.J.
Summer: 70-90 miles a week at 6:30 per mile or faster; typical day—12 miles in 90 minutes or faster.
Early-season: 70-90 a week at 6:00 pace or better; typical day—13 miles in 1:18 or better.
Peak: 70 a week, leaning towards intervals; typical day—3 x 2 miles in 9:50 (on grass), 4 x 1 mile in 4:45.

Mike Cotton, New Canaan High School, New Canaan, Conn.
Summer: 10-15 miles a day—4-5 in morning (7-minute pace), 10-12 in afternoon (6:00-6:30 pace); some racing.
Early-season: 70-85 a week; one day—10 miles at 6:00-6:30 pace or repeat miles at 4:45-5:00.
Peak: 8-10 miles, mostly intervals (every other day); repeat miles or 880-mile-1-1/2 miles-mile-880 progression.

Clancy Devery, South Salem High School, South Salem, Ore.
Summer: Have fun; 100-110 miles a week, maybe an occasional race; no pressure.
Early-season: Build endurance with "hard/easy" program; hard—5 x 1000 meters in 2:44 or fartlek workout; easy—just a plain distance run ("I have over 117 routes").
Peak: Ease up on the distance and do a bit more speedwork and get psyched up; peak lasts only one week and comes only twice in a whole year.

Chris Fox, Martinsburg High School, Martinsburg, W. Va.
Summer: 100 miles a week—5 in morning, 10-12 in evening, at

6:00-6:30 pace.

Early-season: Fartlek over long distance 50% of time, some hills, long runs ("for rest"); fartlek runs are 10 miles with the fartlek part between 300 yards and a mile.

Peak: 20% hills, 70% hard, long runs; 10% speedwork, such as half-mile intervals; one day—5 x one mile under 5:00 with a mile jog between each one.

James Eubank, Clark High School, Las Vegas, Nev.

Summer: 6-10 miles a day at a comfortable pace, with fartlek and hills a couple of times; rest one day a week.

Early-season: 10-15 a day; hills once a week; alternate hard/easy on long runs.

Peak: Speed workouts twice a week with distance afterwards; on other days, only run distance; one day—880s or 440s at race pace, with 6-10 miles afterwards at buildup pace.

Kevin Higdon, Elston High School, Michigan City, Ind.

Summer: Mix long runs with speedwork once a week; one day—13½ miles on roads or bike trails or along beaches on Lake Michigan.

Early-season: Three long runs a week, race once or twice (but run hard only one race); one day—3 in morning, then, in afternoon, 4 warmup, hills, 4 x one mile at 5:20, then two-mile warmdown.

Peak: Cut mileage, run sprint intervals from 440 down; one day—two-mile warmup, stretching, 6 x 110 striding, 4-6 x 440 in 67-70 seconds, two-mile warmdown.

Bob Newark, Red River High School, Grand Forks, N.D.

Summer: two-mile warmup, 8-10 miles hard, mile walk, jog, sprint, two-mile warmdown.

Early-season: two-mile warmup, 10-13 miles, two-mile warmdown.

Peak: Same as early-season with some extra mileage.

Dave O'Conor, Valley Central High School, Montgomery, N.Y.

Summer: Foundation work, easy routine, some road races, go to a cross-country camp.

Early-season: Relaxed distance: controlled hill running. "We must drive five miles to the nearest hill for training."); one day—3-mile warm-up, stretching, 10 x 75-yard accelerations, distance or fartlek, cool down.

Peak: Less volume, more intensity: 3 - 5-mile warmup, stretching, 10-20 75-yard accelerations, 2 sets of 4-5 440's at 60-70 seconds, 4 x 220 at 28-32 seconds, 5-10 x 110 at 13-16 seconds, 2-4 miles cool down.

Scott Reid, Stevenson High School, Stevenson, Wash.

Summer: 9-12 miles a day, speedwork once a week; 6 miles in morning 6 x 880 with 440 jog in between in afternoon.

Early-season: 100 miles a week hard, lots of hillwork; weights three times weekly; one day—3 miles in morning, then weights, 12 miles in afternoon, then 10 x 110-yard hills.

Peak: More quality to simulate racing, with long (15-18) runs on weekends; one day—3 miles in morning; in afternoon, a timed 3-mile run, 4 x 440, 2 x 880, a timed mile.

Thomas Rodenburg, New Ulm High School, New Ulm, Minn.

Summer: Overdistance with no speedwork, increasing to 100 miles in August; one day—10 miles in morning at 7:00 pace, 5 in afternoon at 6:30 pace.

Early-season: Introduce long repetitions of 880 and mile with occasional 220s up a steep hill; aim for 90 miles weekly; on rep day—5 miles at 7:30 pace in morning; in P.M., 2 miles at 7:30, 3 x 1 mile or 8 x 880 and 8 x 220 uphill and 3 miles at 7:00.

Peak: Longer reps of 880s and 440s with increased numbers of flat 220s; still 80-90 a week; one day—5 miles at 7:00 in morning, then 8 miles at 6:00 or reps in evening.

Robert Whetton, Mesa High School, Mesa, Ariz.

Summer: Training at "Runner's Mecca" Camp at 10,000 feet altitude; 5-10 miles in morning, yoga stretching, lift weights religiously ("Yoga has increased my range of motion").

Early-season: High mileage, over 100 a week; we work with electronic pacers: the unit is small and worn on a belt.

Peak: Various distances, uses pacers.

Cliff Wimer, Solanco High School, Quarryville, Pa.

Summer: As much distance as possible for a strong base, 5 miles in morning, 10 in P.M., at good-to-hard pace.

Early-season: Meets Mondays and Thursdays hurt training, if also a Saturday invitational—almost a "lost week"; one day 5 miles in morning, then 10 miles or 6 x 1 mile in P.M.; Saturday—15 miles; Sunday—rest.

Peak: For sharpening; shorten distance but pick up speed; one day—5 x 880 with 3-minute jog in between.

Sometimes, it hurts. Runner Rodenburg volunteers:

"Have suffered two metatarsal stress fractures, both of which took six weeks in a cast to heal. Currently, I am suffering from stress fractures in legs which are not completely healed and give extreme pain in races. Hope to complete the 1976 cross-country season, although it appears somewhat gloomy right now. I was defeated handily in our conference meet by a runner whom I had earlier defeated by 30 seconds.

"In general, I would describe myself as an extremely hard trainer. From time to time, I suffer from various overstress injuries because of this. My most severe month was July, when I went to two running clinics and got in 465 miles for that month, including a 34-mile day. In August, I got a sore thigh and had to lay off a week but still got in 440 miles.

"September and October have been depressing with a great loss of weight (11 pounds), low blood-sugar and a lack of iron, forcing me to feel poorly much of the time. Recently, the legs have become of serious concern and may prove to be an end to the season, but I am *still*

124

training at 85 miles per week and just hoping for the best."

(*Footnote:* Rodenburg led the state's official coaches rankings of top runners for most of the season, then placed only 19th in the state finals after hobbling to the finish line on injured legs. Enough said.)

By and large, these runners use the three-step approach. They tend to differ in the middle phase by starting speedwork in early season, confident that their "1000-mile summers" put them in condition to work at a fast pace even in September. Remember, though, that these runners represent the skimmed top of our champions.

Early speedwork is also given credence by Kim Valentine, a lawyer and longtime runner who has assisted many distance runners in the Greater Boston area. In his book, *Teenage Distance Running,* he outlines a 12-week cross-country training program. There is a gradual mileage reduction, from 86 the first week to 63-1/2 the 12th week. (Sixty-three and a half—does such exactness really help runners, or make them too obsessed with mileage totals to appreciate the sport?)

Valentine's proposed first week:

Monday: Easy 10-mile run to recover from Sunday run.

Tuesday: Twelve-mile steady run with 5 x 300-yard buildups in the middle four miles.

Wednesday: Easy 10-mile run to recover from speedwork.

Thursday: Sixteen miles building evenly from a jog to last mile at 10-mile race pace.

Friday: Eight miles with first mile as warmup, followed by six miles hard, and then jog last mile as warmdown.

Saturday: Ten-mile run with ninth mile hard but not all-out.

Sunday: Twenty miles, or two hours, 30 minutes minimum.

Another step-by-step program is proposed in Don Fuchs' *Pride in a Stride,* billed as a "power-skill training approach to developing cross-country distance runners." Fuchs is a successful coach at Florida's South Plantation High School. He is an advocate of elaborate warmups and exercises, including weight training. He sets his charges running out into the sand and surf, up stadium steps, and over bridges and hills. He divides his season into five phases: summer, pre-school (Aug. 15 to Sept.1), September, October and November. His team's mileage begins at 95 weekly and gradually drops to 58 by season's end. Here is a typical Wednesday in October:

2:15 P.M.: (1) stretch; (2) weight training; (3) 15 minutes on stadium steps; (4) 20 x "running rope"; (5) two-mile cool down.

7 P.M.: (1) jog two-mile warmup; (2) 16 x 330-yards at 54 seconds, jog 110 between each; (3) jog two-mile cool down (total for day—12 miles).

125

And a Wednesday before the district championships in November:

2:15 P.M.: (1) stretch; (2) 10 x "resistance" run circuit (resistance training stresses the driving off running, such as what is done through sand or up hills); (3) jog two-mile cool down.

7 P.M.: (1) stretching; (2) 20 x 150-yard bridge accelerations; (3) jog two-mile cool down (total for day—10 miles).

An example of a more restrained approach is used by Illinois' Deerfield High School, rated the number-one high school cross-country team in the nation for 1976. Coach Len Kusillas tells prospective candidates:

"Basically, our training program is planned so that the athlete experiences a gradual adaptation to stress, and in turn it is our hope that our program develops a greater immunity to fatigue. In the main, our training program consists of slow interval in the early phases, with short recovery, and great quantities of running.

"We make an effort in our training program not to make our daily workouts so exhausting that the athlete finds it difficult for him to recover from day to day. That is one significant reason why the early phases of our program consist of many long runs and interval training, at a pace with a much slower tempo than race pace. In other words, more quantity and less quality.

"We feel that an individual can get in terrific shape by repeat training at fast tempo, but I feel this method of training would create such a strain on the human body that the athlete will not perform up to his potential. Cross-country training success is derived from a long-range goal and not a get-rich-quick philosophy. We gear our program to a graduated stress adaptation plan."

John Goodridge, a former college cross-country coach, conducted a poll of high school team training methods in 1976. Most of the 23 championship-caliber teams from 15 states use the summer as a mileage buildup and progress from moderate to intense speedwork during the regular season. There was a vast range of workload.

From the group, the lightest schedule belonged to Archbishop Ryan, the Philadelphia city champion. Its routine: "Summer running includes 3-12 miles per day gradually increasing through the summer. Early-season work stresses long overdistances of 8-10 miles at medium to hard effort plus fartlek. Mid-season stresses hill work or mile repeats. During peak season, they switch to speedwork of 880s, hill pickups and 1320 time trials. Mileage during season is in the 45-50 range."

126

Fremd High of Illinois, a perennial state-title contender, goes about things differently: "Summer running totals 1000-1200 including a marathon and other long road races. Train three times a day during the season. Three miles in morning plus afternoon and evening workouts. Training method progresses from overdistance to intervals to repetition, with occasional fartlek and speed. Use heavy weights during season. Race twice a week."

Len Kusillas' collegiate counterpart, Coach Ted Banks of 1976 NCAA champion Texas-El Paso, says, "We try to peak for two (cross-country) races—the Western Athletic Conference and, of course, the NCAA."

His system in a nutshell: "We start our team workouts on Aug. 30, the date we register for school. During the first month, we will run about 90 miles a week. We will run intervals maybe once or twice a week, with the emphasis still on quantity. We start our interval work at 75-second (quarter-mile) pace, which would be 30 minutes for six miles. After about 3-4 weeks, depending on the condition of the team, we will start to incorporate some hillwork into our training schedule. We feel this is a very important part of our training. During October, we will drop our (interval) pace to about 73 seconds a lap and start to work on the fast, early pace that is necessary for the NCAA. In November, we cut to a 70-second pace and our mileage drops to 50 weekly, but with good quality."

TRAINING SURVEYS

At the 1974 NCAA championship run in Bloomington, Ind., two pairs of researchers conducted separate surveys in an attempt to determine what, if anything, distinguished the select participants from the mainstream of good, but not great, runners. The methods and conclusions of both studies were published in the September 1975 issue of *Runner's World*.

Carl Foster and Jack Daniels sent questionnaires to all of the 250 finishers. Seventy-seven returned usable replies. Foster and Daniels determined that the average runner of the 77 returnees ran 31:38 for the 10,000-meter race (about 5:05 mile pace for the hilly course); trained 83.9 miles per week during the cross-country season; did 24.4% of their training as interval training and ran 3.05 races of six miles or more prior to the NCAA.

Besides compiling average figures, the writers separated the runners into five categories, based on their performances in the race. Group I runners placed in the top 50, Group II, 51-100, and so on. They concluded:

"Mileage seems to be the most important of the training experience factors. Yet it should be noted that even the Group I runners were averaging only 93 miles per week—a relatively modest figure when compared to the 200-plus miles of the Bedford-Roelants-Lindgren school (Britain's Dave Bedford, Belgium's Gaston Roelants and America's Gerry Lindgren.

"The only other factor of statistical importance was the number of previous six-mile races during the season. The last point refers to the fact that in Group I, runners had experienced 4.73 six-mile races leading up to the NCAA while the last category, Group V, had a figure of 1.08."

This is a revealing statistic, and I was taken aback by it. It suggests that it is crucial for cross-country runners to race frequently at distances at least equal to the distance of the championship meet—regardless of training technique or mileage—if relative success is to be achieved.

It is one thing, in other words, to spill one's guts over four or five miles and quite another to do it over six miles, when in the latter stages there may not be a reserve of guts to spill.

Moreover, does this mean racing experience supersedes training in the degree of impact upon the runner? Perhaps, because the training factors (mileage and intensity) showed no appreciable difference among the groups polled. The racing component did. To rely on this point as fact rather than speculation is hasty, though; similar studies must be performed many times over before we can be absolutely sure.

The other survey was conducted by Tim Gognat and Bob Swank. Having attended the meet, I recall these young men passing out questionnaires to the runners. (Incidentally, this is a marvelous idea. Consider the valuable information just waiting to be plied from a large gathering of superior cross-country runners. Why not have the NCAA Cross-Country Coaches Association—and the NAIA, JUCO, AIAW, etc., even the IAAF—distributes questionnaires at their championships?).

Relative to training, the Gognat-Swank survey brought replies from 74 runners. I'm quoting: "For 67% of the athletes, the typical daily workout distance ranged from 10-15 miles with 76% of the respondents running twice per day. None of those surveyed ran fewer than five miles each day. (Some did only five a day!) Eighty-five per cent ran every day of the week."

Weight work? "Of our sample, 51% answered that they did none,

128

31% replied that they used weights three times a week, and 15% answered once or twice a week." Types of weights? "Thirty-nine per cent went with light weights and a high number of repetitions, 46% used medium weights with a medium number of reps, and 15% lifted heavy weights with few reps."

HILL RUNNING

Sprinkled about our discussions have been some passing remarks about hill running. Mention hill running in the company of coaches is like mentioning abortion in the company of women. People get mad. Some swear by hills, others swear against them or *at* them. Both sides have a pretty good basis for their thinking. Before examining some of the literature, I want to point out that a healthy majority of all of the cross-country people whom I've known endorse forms of hill training. My own experiences have also been mostly positive in this area.

I started running in the spring of 1972. At the time, I lived in Brooklyn, N.Y., hardly a runner's oasis. More than 90% of my mileage was done on flat surfaces. In the fall of 1973, I ran the New York City Marathon, then run at four-plus loops of Central Park's extremely hilly six-mile vehicular route. I was forced to drop out after 20 miles. The pain was excruciating, especially in the lower back area. As my running buddy, Jimmy Behr, might say, even my hair hurt.

A few months later, I moved to hilly Staten Island, where I run at least 50% of my miles on some very rough hills. I ran the New York City Marathon in 1976, and even though it was easier as a new point-to-point course (through all five boroughs), it still contained periodic inclines. The most draining was the one up the decaying Queensborough Bridge, at about the 15-mile point.

You can guess the outcome. While this was the straw that broke many a runner's back, I climbed it easily and ran relatively composed the rest of the way. My time was 3:17, not bad for me, and I definitely attribute my performance to my background on hills.

This anecdote is not all good fortune. I have had my share of injuries, and about half of them have been caused not only by ignorance, impatience and greed, but by ignorance, impatience and greed while running on hills.

There was the time, for example, after a Christmas layoff caused by a skiing vacation, when I decided to make up for lost time. I ran a lot of miles, all on a hilly route. It was very cold. The ground, mostly concrete, was very hard. No warmup, nothing. Just up and out. My right achilles tendon rebelled, and I ended up with severe tendonitis that plagued me for the rest of the winter.

A number of articles have dealt with the whys and wherefores of hill running. Some of them have spouted technical advice geared to *racing*, and I am saving that for the appropriate chapter. Byron Richardson's "A View From The Hill," from the August 1976 *Runner's World*, seems to summarize the prevailing viewpoint. Richardson is a devout hill runner.

He writes, "Hill training, properly applied, can be of great benefit—and not just to a privileged few who have a great deal of leg strength. The problem lies in switching suddenly from flat training to full-scale hill work. The body can't take the sudden change.

"Going up gives anaerobic training without the violent motion of sprinting (and without the boredom of track intervals). It improves the stride. It strengthens two of the basic muscle groups: the quadriceps and the buttocks. Flat training does not get at these muscles. It conditions the cardiovascular system in much the same fashion as interval training. And it gives confidence when hills are encountered during a race.

"Going down forces the runner to concentrate on his stride, and therefore offers a chance to improve it. It gives speedwork without subjecting the body to anaerobic conditions. It gives an opportunity to develop 'leg speed,' the ability to move the legs fast and at the same time stay relaxed. The braking action strengthens the frontal thigh muscles."

But nothing is perfect. Richardson cautions, "Hill training also involves special dangers. There is, first, the ever-present danger of a fall...Good shoes can help you avoid falling. Other violent injuries, such as sprains, are an increased threat, but can also be avoided by watching yourself. More subtle are the dangers involved with the special techniques. Other than actual slipping or falling, these include achilles strain going up, slipping of the foot inside the shoe, flattening (pronation) of the feet and the pounding incurred going downhill."

FOOTING

Proper footwear will minimize these dangers. The athletic shoe industry has been revolutionized in recent years, *vis a vis* running, and protective, quality shoes are not hard to find anymore. Good shoes, of course, are essential for all forms of running. For cross-country, they are the ultimate necessity.

The two most important features of cross-country shoes are sole grip and heel support. The sole must grip the terrain, like the tires on TV commercials, giving you ample traction. This problem is virtually non-existent on the smoothly-paved roads runners tend to frequent. But in the fields, in the thickly-padded land, on uneven ground and up and down the hills, the shoe's sole must work for you, not against you.

Rubber and sponge soles are not the best. Ridged and waffle-type bottoms are much better. I hesitate to endorse a particular shoe. We are all too different in our needs, preferences—and feet. Suffice it to say that Adidas, Puma, Nike and New Balance all have good cross-country shoes in their lines of running footwear. Many runners prefer spiked shoes for cross-country. Usually, the axiom is, the more difficult the terrain, the greater the need for spikes.

Cross-country training takes cross-country running one step further. It does not necessarily make it better. It just adds the dimensions of purpose and preparation, and leads to the next step, cross-country racing.

11
Camping

Every year, after the nation's school doors are shut for a well-deserved two-month breather, thousands of youngsters are temporarily bunked in a sort of supervised wilderness that has become an American sports phenomenon: summer camp.

Most of these are the all-purpose camps, the ones that last up to eight weeks and can be almost as expensive as a year's tuition at a private university. Like the circus, they cater to children of all ages, provide a rainbow of activities, enough food to bloat the world's shot putters and enough athletics to conduct their own Olympics.

These are hideaways for the kids next door, who in later years will delight in recalling the counselors, good and bad, the kid who almost drowned in the lake, the midnight bunk raids, the Big Game, "Color War" and the one girl everybody loved to love in the woods after dark.

These camps have given rise to the specialty camps, where one can cultivate his interest in a particular endeavor from dawn to dusk, usually for segments of a week or two. Much of this genre is comprised of sports camps where authorities and experts will guide you in everything from skiing to sailing, fencing to football, handball to hockey. And running.

Most of the camps that deal with running in one form or another place a lot of emphasis on cross-country. This is so because the scholastic and collegiate fall cross-country seasons follow the period of operation (summer) of these running camps. And since most campers are students (there is a trend, though, in the direction of older campers), it is quite timely to designate cross-country as the major focus of camp. Also, most camps are located in scenic areas of fresh air and wooded trails, and wouldn't it be foolish to narrow the range of a running camp to track events and not capitalize on such surroundings.

Just as interest in running has grown tremendously in the 1970s, so has the number and scope of running camps. Less than a decade ago, there was only a handful of camps because, after all, who wanted to waste time going to a camp just to run? And have to pay for it, yet! In 1976 and 1977, there was a total of at least 44 different running camps serving an annual number of about 5000 athletes.

More camps are apt to follow. Thus far, the camps have mainly served serious *young* runners, those who run almost daily and compete in races. Prospective camp owners will soon start to tap the public at large. There are millions of runners, or joggers, whose reliance on the sport is not to run marathons or train 10 miles a day but to run occasionally, lose weight, keep fit and feel better suited for their all-important matches in tennis and softball. Fine.

An attempt to move in this direction was made by the Athletic Attic Family Running Camp. Marty Liquori, the world-class runner and athletic shoe entrepreneur; Barry Brown, another champion runner and attorney, and Hal Higdon, the noted Masters runner and author, combined energies early in 1977 and formed a running camp with a family concept.This was to be a one-week camp in early August, located in the Adirondack Mountains of New York, but administrative problems forced cancellation of the 1977 program. The trio hopes to return in 1978. (For information: Athletic Attic, 1135-E N.W. 23rd Avenue, Gainesville, Fla. 32601.)

Running camps generally fall into the following categories: track and field, track and cross-country, distance running, cross-country. The last two labels are virtually synonymous. There are several factors that should be of major interest to anyone considering a camp: location, features and facilities, date, cost, eligibility, emphasis and staff.

Many camps are situated on grounds used by all-purpose camps, whose facilities have been vacated by departing youngsters. Some are spread out on the campus of schools or universities. Others have their own setups, which may be used for such things as seminars, clinics and retreats when not for camp.

The facilities and features range from modest to extensive—i.e., from just the basic running territory and spartan existence to swimming, gym use, campfire outings, lectures, socials and the like. Most are held in August, the month likely to attract the greatest number of campers. July is second; a few camps operate in June. The cost per week, including lodging and meals, runs between $75 and $150. Eligibility? Some camps are restrictive with regard to sex or age or student status.

The emphasis of a camp is directly related to its staff. If champion pole vaulters or sprinters, or their coaches compose the personnel, cross-country runners would do well to go elsewhere. Track and field camps that boast also of cross-country would be hard-pressed to do both, unless sufficiently staffed with distance-oriented people.

Some camps come across very well in this department. Athletes of Olympic stature and renowned coaches lecture, give instruction and participate with the campers. Another type of emphasis, which is connected to location, is high altitude. There are a few camps in the Rockies and farther west that place runners at 8000 feet altitude or above. There are enormous benefits to accrue from such running, but inexperienced campers without a strong foundation of heavy mileage are advised to approach altitude training cautiously. One of these camps, located in Brianhead, Utah, is called Runner's Mecca, and judging from its popularity, its name is not unfounded.

Eastward, the most ambitious camp appears to be the Stroudsburg camp in Pennsylvania. In 1976, its three weekly sessions drew a total of 400 teenaged campers. Twice, I have appeared at the camp and delivered what would loosely be called a speech to a packed barn of eager listeners. I also ran there and toured the grounds.

The atmosphere was congenial and relaxed, and everyone seemed to be having a good time. The highlight of the week was an informal cross-country race; that is, a race-swim. At the end of three miles of running, the campers were obliged to rip off their shoes and swim a few hundred yards across the lake to the finish line. Eventually, even the bystanders got a rinsing.

Camp is a business, managed usually by coaches seeking to supplement their regular income. As in other businesses, there are financial peaks and pitfalls. There are factors of labor, overhead, supply and demand, competitiveness and managerial supervision. Some camps close before they even open. Others turn away applicants. All this benefits prospective campers. To survive and prosper, camps will have to offer more and more, and at reasonable rates.

Be glad for this system. There are liberties. In some European nations, youngsters with athletic potential are plucked from their habitat and placed into camps of "athletic culture." Don't bet on finding any swim-runs or late-night jam sessions over there.

Is running camp for you? Probably. If your reasons for wanting to go match the features and the objectives of the camps, then there will be a compatible relationship. But camps don't perform miracles. Marginally skilled runners will not emerge from camp as champions. Camp is not a place for a crash course in high mileage. Camp is a place to soak up some nice, comfortably long workouts, receive top-level instruction from knowledgeable coaches, bask in the camaraderie of runners, cool out at a shaded lake and surface better prepared, emotionally and physically, for upcoming cross-country season.

There are certain precautions. If you have been running 50 miles a week in July and enter camp in August, don't feel compelled to jump into groups of athletes running two or three times a day and logging 20 miles or more. You may also confront abundant hill work, a weight program and all the food and drink you want. Moderation is the keynote. How ironic it would be to acquire an injury or gain weight at the very place you sought to elevate, not deteriorate, your conditioning.

Listed below, alphabetically, are all of the camps that advertised in American running publications in 1976 and '77. This list is virtually complete, since to become a viable enterprise a camp has to promote itself in the running press. A few of these entries may not be operating any more, having closed after the '76 season. Each camp is listed with its address, director, eligibility and emphasis. There is no need to list the dates, staff and costs because those factors are variable. Up-to-date information can be obtained from the latest camp brochures.

RUNNING CAMPS

All-American Cross-Country Camp. Bill Squires, director. Cross-country. Grades 9 and up. P. O. Box 5021, Roxbury Crossing, Mass. 02120. Boys only.

Bear Backers Track and Field Camp. MGB, director. All track and field events. Male and female, 9-19. Intercollegiate Athletics, Univ-California, Berkeley, Calif.

Bill Bowerman Camp. Bill Bowerman, director. Cross-country and distance running. Male and female, all ages. Sunriver, Ore. 97701.

Blue Mountain Sports Camps. John Covert, director. Cross-country. Male and female, 13-19. Onawa Lodge, Box 198, Mountainhome, Pa. 18042.

Blue Ridge Trails. Bill Keesling, director. Middle- and long-distance running. Male and female, all ages. Box 28544, Furman University, Greenville, S.C. 29613.

Can-Am International Training Site. Dave Aungier, director. Track and field and cross-country. Male and female, 12-17. Tully, N.Y. 13159.

Camp Casey. Ken Foreman, director. All events. Male and female, junior high through college. Seattle Pacific College, Seattle, Wash.

Catoctin Cross-Country Camp. Jeff Whitmore, director. Cross-country. Male and female, 12-18. 32 Clearwater Court, Damascus, Md. 20750.

Clear Lake Cross-Country Camp. Art Hutton, director. Cross-country, middle- and long-distance. Male and female high school students. 304 Stanley Blvd., Yakima, Wash. 98902.

Colorado Adventuring Distance Running Camp. Bill Crowell, director. Cross-country and general conditioning. Male and female, all ages. Box 293, Westcliffe, Colo. 81252.

Conestoga Camp. Mike Garcia, director. Cross-country and distance running. Boys and girls. Minerva, Ohio. 44657.

Empire Track and Field Camp. Louise Mead Tricard, director. All track and field events. Girls only, ages 12 through college. 17 Walnut Hill Road, Poughkeepsie, N.Y. 12603.

Florida Distance Camp. Roy Benson, director. Middle and long distance running. Male and female, 10 and up. Athletic Department, Univ.-Florida, Gainesville, Fla. 32604.

Green Mountain Cross-Country Camp. Peter Davis, director. Cross-country and middle- and long-distance running. Male and female, 12-20. Lyndon Center, Vt.

High-Altitude Training Camp. Don McMahill, director. Distance training. Male and female, 12 and up. Cheyenne Family YMCA, 1401 Dunn Ave., Cheyenne, Wyo. 82001.

Connecticut Cross-Country Camp. Mr. Haley, director. Cross-country. 45 Birchbank, Shelton, Ct. 06484.

High Sierra Running Camp. Tom Feroah, director. High altitude training. Male and female, all ages. 1264 N. Sierra, Reno, Nev. 89503.

Jayhawk Track & Field Camp. Gary Pepin, director. All track and field events. Boys and girls, 13-17. Track Office, Univ.-Kansas, Lawrence, Kans. 66044.

Jim Bush Track & Field Camp. Jim Bush, director. All track and field events. Male and female, 10-18. 405 Hilgard, Los Angeles, Calif. 90024.

Jim Ryun Running Camps. Directors at four different sites. Boys and girls, 10-18. P.O. Box 6266, Santa Barbara, Cal. 93111.

Jerry Quiller Copper Mountain Distance Camp. Jerry Quiller, director. High-altitude distance training. Male and female, all ages. P.O. Box 1, Copper Mountain, Colo. 80443.

Marist College Distance Running Camp with Marty Liquori. Rich Stevens, director. Cross-country and distance running. Boys and girls, 7th to 12 grade; men and women, college and up. Track Office, Marist College, Box 814, Poughkeepsie, N.Y. 12601.

Mel Pender Track & Field Development Camp. Mel Pender, director. All track and field events. Boys and girls, 8 to 18, and college athletes. Butler Street YMCA, 22 Butler Street, N.E., Atlanta, Ga. 30303.

Michigan State Cross-Country Camp. Jim Gibbard, director. Cross-country. Boys and girls, ages 12 to high school senior. Track Office, Jenison Field House, Michigan State University, East Lansing, Mich. 48824.

Mid-Atlantic Running Camp. Browning Ross, director. All forms of running. Male and female, ages 10 through high school and up. Sports East, 240 S. Broad St., Woodbury, N.J. 08096.

Montecito-Sequoia Running Camp. Steve Lieurance, director. Distance running and general conditioning. Male and female, all ages. 1485 Redwood Drive, Los Altos, Cal. 94022.

New England Track & Field Camp. Norm Levine and Joe Donahue, directors. All events. Boys and girls. P.O. Box 359, Scituate, Mass. 02066.

Oklahoma State Cross-Country Camp. Cross-country. High school boys and girls, 14-18. Track Office, Gallagher Hall, Oklahoma State University, Stillwater, Okla. 74074.

Olympia Sport Village. Thomas Rosandich, director. Track and field and cross-country. Boys and girls 12-19. Upson, Wisc. 54564.

Phidippides Summer Trails. Jeff Galloway, director. Cross-country and distance running. Male and female, all ages. 1544 Piedmont Rd., N.E., Atlanta, Ga 30324.

Roy Chernock Cross-Country Camp. Roy Chernock, director. Cross-country and distance running. Male and female, junior high and high school students. 36 Lake Lane, Princeton, N.J. 08540.

Runner's Alternative. Topper Powers, director. General running. Male and female, all ages. 2002 W. Middlefield, Mountain View, Calif. 94040.

Runner's Mecca. Richard Heywood, director. High-altitude distance training. Male and female, all ages. Box 2186, Mesa, Ariz. 85204.

Rutgers Track and Cross-Country Camps. Frank Gagliano, director. Cross-Country and track and field. Boys and girls, 12-17. Rutgers University, Track Office, Intercollegiate Athletics, New Brunswick, N.J. 08903.

Southeast Women's Track Camp. Jerry Smith, director. All track and field events. Females only, 13 and up. 1027 Sanders Street, Auburn, Ala. 36830.

Sports Acres Track and Cross-Country Camps. Harry Johnson, director. Distance running and field events. Boys and girls, 9-19. Box 8488, Portland, Ore. 97207.

Stroudsburg Cross-Country Camp. Jim Smith, director. Cross-Country. Male and female, 10 and up. 229 Rocky Point Landing Road, Rocky Point, N.Y. 11778.

Symposium on Running. Fred Hardy, director. Middle- and long-distance running. Male and female, all ages. Box 6, University of Richmond, Richmond, Va. 23173.

Tahoe Trails. Jeff Galloway, director. High-altitude and distance training. Men and women, all ages. Phidippides, 1544 Piedmont Rd., N.E., Atlanta, Ga 39324.

Ted Banks Track & Field Camp. Ted Banks, director. All track and field events. Boys and girls, ages 10 through high school. Cross-country, too. 6619 Los Altos, El Paso, Texas 79912.

Westminister-Jimmy Carnes Track Camp. Jimmy Carnes, director. All track and field events. Male and female, 8-18. 1135 N.W. 23rd Avenue, Gainesville, Fla.

White Mountain Sports Camp. Dick Dow, director. Cross-country. Boys and girls, 12-18. 52 Hayward Road, Acton, Mass. 01720.

Wildcat Track Camp. Deloss Dodds, director. All track and field events. Boys and girls, ages 8 through high school. 1613 Virginia Drive, Manhattan, Kans.

Wisconsin Camp of Champions. Dan McClimon, director. Track and field and distance running. Boys and girls, junior high and high school students. 428 Virginia Terrace, Madison, Wisc. 53705.

Wolfpack Cross-Country Camp. James Westcott, director. Middle- and long-distance running. Male and female, ages 12 through high school. Athletic Department, North Carolina State University, Raleigh, N.C. 27607.

It is a healthy list. It is very important to note that the addresses given are not, in most cases, the specific site of the camp but the contact for the camp's director. For example, Jeff Galloway's Tahoe Trails is located in the Lake Tahoe region, not in Atlanta; Rich Heywood's Runner's Mecca is located in Brianhead, Utah, not in Arizona; Jim Smith's Stroudsburg Camp is in Pennsylvania, not in New York.

Thinking of the offerings of these camps and their primary attraction to the young, I almost wish I could start my youth all over again. Someday I might even develop my own camp. Then, I would have an excuse for being a kid once more.

12
Healing

My first visit with Doc Goldstein was in June 1974. I had fallen from a chair at work and severely bruised my right hip. I couldn't walk, much less run. Even with a cane, the pain was piercing.

I had never been to a chiropractor before but knew of Doc Goldstein. Many running and coaching acquaintances of mine relied on him and drew relief from their disappointments just because they knew he was available. They would speak of him in mystical terms, as though by merely meeting him one's troubles would be over.

It surprised me then to find Doc Goldstein a most ordinary-*looking* man. He is middle-aged, stocky, balding and unstylishly dressed. One would expect to find him selling shoes to bratty kids and escaping for two weeks every year to the shores of Miami Beach. He answers his own phone. He has a waiting room that seats nine persons so tightly that if all nine stretched their legs they would all cross in the middle of the room. His voice has concern but not authority. He is unassuming and unpretentious. He has performed miracles with some patients—not only medical ones—but prefers to stay away from the glory, gaining satisfaction in the knowledge of his contributions and in the friends he makes.

When I hobbled into his Brooklyn office that summer day, I was more concerned with loss of running time than of possible damage to my hip. Doc told me I'd be walking normally in two weeks and running in three weeks. I did not believe him. He came very close. I was jogging in a month and running 50 miles a week by the end of summer.

Since I started running in the spring of 1972, I have suffered through a number of injuries, most of which could have been avoided with some restraint—the runner's most useful preventive tool. Restraint is something acquired with maturity; that is why some people never find it. But as Dr. George Sheehan, the renowned running physician, says, when we run we are like children. We do not know when to stop. Even if we know when we have had enough, we go back for more.

During the first few years of my running, I did very little exercising. No stretching, no calisthenics. My muscle tone in some areas was flimsy. I was running a lot of miles, but my body was susceptible to the onslaught of ailments. Simple laziness. Now I exercise religiously, before and after running. This is by no means a panacea, but it has helped, and I'll explain how shortly.

There was the time it was pouring rain, and I did an indoor workout up and down the apartment house stairway. There were seven flights. I did about 20 sets. My right achilles tendon rightfully rebelled. Another time, after a short layoff, I ran a lot of hills in cold weather without any warmup. My left achilles tendon rebelled. On another occasion, I picked up shin splints the same way—too much running in conditions my body was not ready for.

I have also contracted "runner's knee." After one very busy March, an early spring Saturday dawned bright and beautiful, so I thought I would make up for lost time by putting in an 18-miler. That smart move cost me an entire spring of running.

I once stepped in a hole and nearly broke a toe: more layoff.

Marathon races have left me with groin, back and hamstring problems, all of which subsided in due time.

Recently, I tripped on an uneven sidewalk and needed stitches to sew up a punctured vein in my left elbow. I didn't lose any running time, but it hurt like hell.

"Aren't you going to give me some kind of anesthetic?" I asked the doctor.

"No," he said, "for this you don't need it." Sure. He gave me three stitches "cold." It hurt so much I was actually laughing.

To clarify a few terms briefly, the achilles tendon is a thin cord that connects the heel bone with the calf muscle and takes its name from

Greek mythology. A noted physician once told me that in some persons these tendons are strong and rope-like, and in others (like me) they are thin and string-like. When they are excessively stretched in the course of running, irritation and inflammation can result. You will occasionally hear of a football quarterback who cannot walk because of a *torn* achilles tendon which requires surgery.

Shin splints cause pain along the front of the lower leg. When I had it, the tendon adjacent to the shin bone was irritated and swollen a bit and I could place a finger on the exact spot of pain. There can be several causes of shin problems. I was told that I had an imbalance in the muscular strength between the front and back of the leg.

Runner's knee is technically known as chondromalacia, which sounds like a plague—and in a sense it is one among distance runners. There are many kinds of knee injuries and many reasons for them. There is a school of thought gaining popularity that claims that knee problems are really foot problems and knee ailments will persist unless the foot is properly treated. This happened in my case.

The podiatrist ascertained that my feet had an imbalance, causing them to strike the ground not squarely but on a distinct angle. When running, this, in turn, caused the cartilage in my knee to rotate and become irritated. The doctor took a mold of my foot, as a dentist will do for braces, and designed a pair of lightweight inserts to plug up the imbalance and square off my foot plant. I was running in a week without pain, and my knees have not bothered me since.

For my array of injuries, I have seen Doc Goldstein, whose full name is Seymour Mac Goldstein; Dr. James Shea, an orthopedist and marathon runner, and Dr. Richard Schuster, who discovered my foot disorder. Dr. Shea has returned to his native New Hampshire because of his skyrocketing malpractice insurance rates in New York. Dr. Schuster, a podiatrist affiliated with a New York City medical school, maintains an office and laboratory in Queens where he treats mostly runners, more than 3000 of them by now.

These men, to their credit, have never prescribed for me that four-letter word: rest. While under their care, I have been told to slow down and run less but never to forego running completely. However, the running patient hears his body signals even louder that the physician. Most of my injuries were cured with a combination of proper treatment—and total rest. Many times I forced myself not to run a step for up to a month. It was the only thing that worked.

Doc Goldstein speaks of the prevalence of certain types of injuries as though there is a pattern to them. As a beautician might say, "We're doing a lot of shags and Afro cuts," or a carpenter might say, "We're doing a lot of bookcases and patio decks," Doc Goldstein, with a turned eyebrow and lines of worry on his forehead, says, "We're doing a lot of ankles and hamstrings now."

There are patterns to injuries, patterns that depend mainly on the weather and the season. There are tendencies apparent to Goldstein during every cross-country season. In the fall, much of his time is devoted to backs, ankles, knees, shins and achilles tendons.

Generally, Doc Goldstein claims, a runner is apt to incur injury if his spinal and pelvic areas are not balanced and squared off. If one's right side is "higher" than the left side, for example, the shock of running will be absorbed in an uneven manner. This tendency is magnified during cross-country because of murderous hills, bumpy terrain and aggressive racing. He also states that many injuries come about because the overall muscle tone of the body is weak, and the runner is unprepared for the stress of hard cross-country activity.

In the fall, Goldstein sees many runners with lumbosacral strain, or pain in the lower back. They "drive" uphill, making their weak muscles work inordinately hard. They are not in very good shape when they hit the hills. A healthy amount of pushups and situps will develop the abdomen and upper torso, thus taking some of the pressure away from the back and enabling the body to function more efficiently. Some light weight repetitions may also be helpful. These are preventive measures. Treatment might include warm showers to relax the musculature. Run lightly, but stay away from hills.

Ankle problems pass through Doc Goldstein's purview. On cross-country ground, the foot plant is erratic. The ankle sometimes "goes under" or is "jammed." There is swelling, tissue tear or possible broken blood vessels. Shoes with a solid heel counter give much-needed security to the ankle. Doc Goldstein gives some runners a foam wedge as an insert to stablize the area further. Damaged ankles should always be checked for all movement, lateral and vertical—or what doctors call flexion and extension, inversion and eversion.

If achilles tendons are not overly stretched on the uphills, then they may be jammed by the downhill pounding when we "brake" instead of letting loose. (This braking motion can also irritate hamstring muscles.) In cross-country racing, there frequently is not even a clear path down hills, causing us not only to brake but to brake while off balance. This can cause soreness in the delicate tendons. Wall pushups will give them more elasticity, making them more flexible for the tasks of cross-country.

142

Hills also can play with knees when the quadriceps muscles are not in proper tone. Strong quadriceps—the front part of the leg above the knee—serve to stablize the knee and prevent a pinching of the cartilage.

"The largest percentage of injuries are incurred in practice, not competition," says Doc Goldstein, who, again, is not an advocate of total rest. If a runner does no running while an injury is healing and being treated, Goldstein says, when he resumes active running his entire body will not be ready for the stress and additional injury will result.

"My average runner, even with a hamstring pull, is back running in 10 days," says Goldstein, boasting not of himself but of the athletic approach to injury. But that's not the only reason hundreds of runners keep his office open as much as 14 hours a day, seven days a week. More on that later.

The phenomenon of sports medicine, although very new in the field of health, is gaining momentum. Medical schools are paying it more than lip service. Professional journals are studying it. More physicians are heeding its call. In the forefront of this movement is Dr. George Sheehan, a 59-year-old New Jersey cardiologist, marathon runner, lecturer, columnist, author and father of 12 children. He is the author of the widely-acclaimed *Dr. Sheehan on Running* and is medical editor of *Runner's World*. At times, he has been critical of the medical profession in general, and of conventional prognoses and treatment in particular.

He insists, "My relationship to sports medicine has been as an athlete rather than as a doctor."

Dr. Sheehan writes, "We are dealing in problems measured in millimeters. Often, the injury is precipitated by wear of the regular running shoe down to a critical point—the heel, for instance, where an eighth of an inch makes a difference. Use of a totally new type of shoe for a major effort will also bring on difficulties, as will change of surfaces and even change of direction when there is a slant in the road.

"I cannot emphasize too strongly that this is a structural, almost architectural, problem, not a medical one. You would almost be better off in the hands of an engineer than a doctor when these illnesses strike. At least you would not have your problem complicated by medication which in the long run will do no good. What the runner needs is to be restored to structural balance. Acupuncture, surgery or wonder drugs will not do that."

A four-year *Runner's World* survey indicates that injuries to the knee, achilles tendon and shins occur most frequently among runners. They are followed by injuries to the ankle, heel, arch, calf, hip, hamstring and forefoot. In an article on "First Aid For The Injured" (July 1977 *RW*), many of Dr. Sheehan's favorite exercises were endorsed as preventive measures. Sheehan's "Magic Six" includes wall pushups, bent-leg situps and hamstring stretches.

Another person concerned with running injury is Harry Groves, the cross-country and track coach at Penn State University and past president of the NCAA Cross-Country Coaches Association. Groves also is not an outsider looking in. He is an active marathon runner and in the over-40 class regularly breaks the three-hour mark. In an article in *The Harrier*, Groves addressed himself to cross-country injuries as they relate to school-affiliated runners and their intense season.

"When it comes to training and racing," he writes, "the athlete must do a certain quantity of training and engage in a certain number of competitions to develop top performance. In this situation, the coach often feels that 'you are damned if you do' train intensely and 'damned if you don't.' Either way may cause success. However, hard, intense work and numerous races are gambles to the future of your athlete. The purpose of this article is to suggest some preventive and remedial actions in order to bring your athlete to his 'big day' physically healthy and injury free."

Here is Groves' 14-point program:

1. If you are after high volume mileage, make it moderate. It will pay big dividends over the months.

2. Carry a training cycle over more than one year with some meets as an incentive to keep going.

3. Take age and development level into account when setting up a training program.

4. Try to take easy days or moderate days at least four days a week. For young athletes, there should only be one or two days a week of hard training.

5. Morning runs are easy runs with only more developed athletes taking them (in addition to the regularly-scheduled workout). A 30-minute run at 7:00 mile pace is adequate for young athletes.

6. Be careful of constant hard interval track training along with frequent hard downhill running. These two workouts often do more harm than good when done too much or too fast.

7. Take a day of very hard training every week followed by an easy day of off-the-track training.

8. Do weight training of 10 reps for the entire body three days a week in development season and two days a week in competitive season. This will strengthen the muscles and the joints.

9. Knee extensions or quadriceps curls are a must to prevent knee pains and injuries associated with the kneecap and surrounding tissue. Do these three days a week, starting at 20-pound lifts, doing 10 times each leg separately. On the last rep, hold to a count of 10. Go up in weight as strength increases. Sixty pounds is a good general strength level to stabilize.

10. Along with the knee extensions, hamstring curls will act to prevent injury when running faster in late season. The hamstring injuries occur as a result of an imbalance in the quad/hamstring ratio. This means only that the *ratio* is out of balance. Begin with 10 pounds and do 10 reps on each leg separately.

11. Muscle testing, particularly in the foot extensors and flexion, quadriceps, hamstrings and thighs will determine possible areas for future breakdown. At present, we are working in this area to determine minimum strength requirements. If the muscle areas are weak, then a corrective program will be initiated as an injury preventive.

12. Flexibility work in all joints including the back will serve as a great preventive.

13. Care of footwear is important. Many injuries to knees and hips can be attributed to the wearing off of heels or sides of shoes or to the interior of the shoes. At least two pairs or preferably four pairs in use at one time will help athletes with a tendency toward injury.

14. Prolonged fatigue from improper training lowers resistance. Lowered resistance is an invitation to illness.

Doc Goldstein's office walls are decorated with plaques given to him in tribute from his patients. One, from the Heart & Soul Track Club, is inscribed: "In appreciation of service to the metropolitan area track community." His shelves are filled with dozens of medals and trophies of all description won by athletes who limped into his office moaning, "Doc, I gotta run. I gotta win." Many times they did, and they gave their awards to Doc Goldstein and told him, "You keep this, Doc, you really won it."

Maybe that's why he does it: the small tokens of gratitude from needy people, most of them young, impoverished and black, who cling to running as the avenue for a better life.

Doc Goldstein has been a chiropractor for 25 years. About 50% of his patients are runners. He treats other athletes, from football players to ice skaters, swimmers to gymnasts. He treats whole teams such as the Atoms Track Club or D.C. Striders as though he were a permanent staff member. He has been the attending doctor at track meets like the

145

Millrose Games and Colgate Women's Games, the latter requiring his all-day presence at 10 days worth of qualifying rounds that had a record entry of 17,000.

He has treated some of the nation's finest runners, Cheryl Toussaint, Robin Campbell and Mattline Render among the women, and Steve Williams, Vinnie Matthews, Byron Dyce and Mike Sands among the men. They call him from distant parts of the country to chat and get advice. His phone is always on the hook and his office is always open.

"I worked on Vinnie every day for three weeks before the '72 Olympic Trials," recalls Goldstein. "Hamstring pulls. Back." Matthews made the US team and won the gold medal in Munich in the 400 meters.

Doc Goldstein's demeanor is even and subdued, his manner is reassuring, and his concern is genuine. His care is total. Not all of his patients pay him. Some bring school insurance forms from which Goldstein is never reimbursed in full. Some bring tales of woe that mean: small as his fee is, they just ain't got the money. They play no games with him. The word is out. They know he's straight. No strings attached.

"I let them slide," says Goldstein. "Either their parents don't care, or they can't afford it."

So they travel the buses and subways from black neighborhoods to Goldstein's office near the east end of Brooklyn's Flatbush Avenue.

"Sometimes," says Goldstein, "I've even got to give them money to get home." He laughs. "But every kid you save, you're saving a human being. A lot of them would fall out of track otherwise. What is it worth? It's a labor of love."

Once, when Goldstein himself required surgery to correct an abdominal disorder, his schedule was thrown out of whack for 10 days. "When I came back, they were lined up out in the street," he recalls. He means it.

"I'm their Father Confessor. They have no one else to talk to. There's a lot of stuff they tell me I can't tell you."

Goldstein will always be in "business," for there will always be young runners to be saved. Are their injuries inevitable? Yes, says *Runner's World* editor Joe Henderson:

"As long as runners run at or past their limits, they'll get hurt. And if we didn't push our limits, we wouldn't be runners."

13
Racing

Craig Virgin: "I'm a more complete runner now. I've been practicing different strategies each race, knowing one of them would pay off here...Rose pulled four moves in the middle. He'd spurt and take off. He's a good hill runner. He was cagey. He couldn't break me. There was a lot of pushing and shoving. Very physical. Elbows. Once I had to grab him and push him aside. At the fifth mile, he took off downhill. Tried to jump me. But I stayed with him. Then, I powered up the last hill and beat him to the top by a step."

Nick Rose: "I took off at two (miles) and Craig was still there. I tried to break him on the hills, but at four he was still there. I tried getting him at five. He had a great run, no mistakes."

Welcome to cross-country. The racing part. The desultory mellowness of a morning's cross-country outing is shattered when you choose to stand up and be counted. The natural decor is no longer captivating. Neither is it capitulating, for when the gun sounds it is not just you and it, but you and it—and many others. There is something primitive about 100 persons racing over the countryside.

Craig Virgin and Nick Rose know all about this. They are cross-country veterans and runners of the highest order. Their comments were made in November 1975, moments after the NCAA championship run on the Penn State University golf course in University Park. Virgin, a handsome Illinois junior who looks the male counterpart of the All-American Breck Girl, outfoxed the crafty Rose, a Western Kentucky senior by way of Great Britain. Rose, the defending champion, acquired his cunning on the madhouse English cross-country circuit.

One would think that the gifted Virgin, who made the 1976 US Olympic team in the 10,000 meters, would not feel compelled to make extra preparation in his bid for the NCAA crown. Raw talent, dedicated training, vast experience—what a potent mixture! But, alas, that one elusive ingredient was not yet brought to a boil. That was the strategy, the nuts-and-bolts wherewithal, to meet a shrewdy such as Rose on his own terms and dethrone him with a bag of tricks that would make a Halloween goblin green with envy.

Virgin admits he came up with the proper balance of keen tactics and hard running. By accident? Well, it can happen, but Craig planned for it. Stung by his 12th place the year before when he was also co-favored—"I humiliated myself"—Virgin decided to use the races leading up to the NCAA as a testing ground.

Although facing tough opposition in the Midwest, where cross-country is not taken lightly, Craig felt confident enough to give various strategies the onceover. One meet, he'd start out fast; the next, he'd throw in a fast mile in the middle, working different combinations, not only to judge his own success but to gauge the reactions of the other competitors. He won every race comfortably.

We are not all as fortunate as a Craig Virgin or Nick Rose. We are not nearly good enough to play around with our strengths and weaknesses, refining them to blot out the margin for error. We are not in the position to contend for a national championship. At least most of us aren't. But to strive for what we can do in cross-country races, even we can learn from Virgin and Rose.

The distinctions regarding runner's intentions in the chapter on training are unnecessary for racing. Training is a lengthy, ongoing process that cannot be attacked in the same manner by runners of diverse ability, experience and intent. Racing is more an episode than a process. It is much the same for everyone. It is an entity unto itself, and whether you are a prince or a pauper, racing cross-country well will depend on several indisputable factors.

First, to emphasize the duties of the job, consider that in road running it is rare that the runner has more to deal with than how fast he can travel over a given route. Now that it quite a lot to deal with, but corss-country has that much and more. It is multi-dimensional. Often, for example, there are lots of people and little room. There is not the streamlined sterility of a clothesline of runners strung out on evenly-laid roads.

My points about racing are tailored to the individual, not the team since the team dynamics of cross-country are dealt with elsewhere. I also try to restrict my comments here to cross-country and not go on to other forms of racing, except for reasons of comparison and illumination. Furthermore, any type of racing drips with heavy psychological overtones, and I do not wish to say whether one's love of Mother and Apple Pie will have any bearing on racing performance.

When I ran high school cross-country in the early 1960s, the coach gave us only three tokens of advice about racing. I'm paraphrasing: When going uphill, shorten your stride and pump your arms; when you pass someone, pass him good; when it really hurts, relieve the pain by not thinking about it—instead think about something totally different like pickles and sex. Since I rarely passed anyone or made it up hills very well, guess what I had on my mind in the fall of '63.

We've come a long way, baby. Here are 10 rules guaranteed to make you forget all about pickles, but not about sex.

1. INTRACOURSE

Get a course map, but don't rely only on it. I am not good at discerning maps, just as I am not good at tuning up my car or wiring stereo units. Don't depend, either, on persons familiar with the route telling you all about it. That's like the directions you get in a strange town. People who live there unconsciously assume you know certain things and neglect to tell you about the ol' fork in the road.

The only way really to know a course is to see it for yourself. Traveling teams usually arrive the day before a meet and take a run-through as part of a pre-race tuneup. If you are at the race site only a couple of hours before the gun, you may not be inclined even to jog the *entire* course. Look at part of it at least.

Be alert, observant, analytical. Where are the hills and the other obstacles? How is the footing? Where are the narrow passages? Are there woods to counteract the wind? How long are the opening and closing sections? Is the route clearly marked? Where are the "blind" stretches that will shield the leaders from your view? Are there alternative paths? Sharp turns?

149

You have to be ready for anything, especially since some runners always have a home-course advantage. When that is you, capitalize on it. If you do not know the course, your attentions will be diverted, and you will fall victim to unsuspected circumstances.

In 1975, I ran a two-mile cross-country race at Van Cortlandt Park in New York City. I knew just how the opening "flats" would be and could pace my start well. I was familiar with the bumpy "cowpath" and Cemetery Hill and the suddenness of the final straightaway. I knew when to press and when to give. I ran well—but not that well—and outclassed my far superior running partner, Jimmy Behr, who had never seen the course before. He was dumbfounded by the flying start taken by some of the runners and the hazards of Cemetery, a hill without a gilded edge to it.

2. WHO'S WHO

Is it the kind of field in which you should be able to run up front with the heavies, or one in which you'd best be reserved and let the others control the action? Know your opposition—its general makeup and whether or not the crazy guy who takes off like a sprinter is really crazy or the race favorite.

In many cases, the other runners function as your guide. This is not a 440-yard track, and usually there is no coach to call off split times. Course variations sometimes render exact pace judgments impossible. If your less-accomplished teammate is way ahead of you after the first mile, you'd better pick up the pace in the next mile. You're lagging. If you're feeling half-baked with three quarters of the race to go, glance at the guy next to you. If he's the same one who took last week's race in record time, maybe you'd better ease up before it's too late. The latter example does not subdue competitiveness or repress high hopes. If you feel the proverbial second-wind later on, by all means go with your instincts.

3. FOXY LADY

And foxy man. Runners beware and be foxy. In cross-country the shortest distance between two points is not always a straight line. It is the quickest line. There is more than one way to dodge a tree, skim a stream, take a turn and clear a hurdle. Will you leap over a puddle or go around it or through it? I've seen runners try and avoid water as if it were the plague. So what if you get wet (except when the temperatures are low). You take water the fastest way, not the neatest way. Cross-country is for the hearty.

Negotiating turns is something few runners give much thought to.

Hal Higdon has given it a lot of thought, and in the September 1976 *Runner's World* wrote, "By taking turns properly, you sometimes can gain a half-stride or more on your opponent, which may be critical in a tactical race."

Higdon advises, "Several strides before you reach your turn, you place your upper body in a sideways motion: outside shoulder forward, inside shoulder back, outside arm raised, inside arm down. As you reach the turn, you lean and bring your legs into alignment with your shoulders, allowing yourself to 'fall' around the turn, at the same time propelling yourself around it."

This sounds like the game plan for an end sweep in football. But Higdon, who has been running around the world for 30 years, is a master tactician, so try his turn recipe and adapt it to your needs.

4. IF HE HOLLERS, LET HIM GO

Let him go—by surging ahead of him. This brings me back to my high school coach. When you are going to pass an opponent, do it convincingly. Don't dawdle. Open up and move out. He will feel more defeated, and you will feel more encouraged to pass the next runner. This tone may smack of nastiness, but cross-country racing is no place for niceties.

The camaraderie of road racing is well documented. Marathon men chatting, exchanging advice, pulling each other along. Cross-country runners are pretty sweet themselves, but if you wince at the idea of "running down" opponents, take comfort in the thought that they will be trying to do the same thing to you. If you sense that happening to you, seize the chance to increase your pace—unless it's too early in the race or your energy is already too spent. If it is a team race, valuable points are involved in this sort of give-and-take.

This technique can also be applied when you have been running side-by-side with a competitor for a while. When you sense him weakening, take off. You'll be gone.

Staten Island, N.Y., schoolboys Marty Walsh and Don Perrina were running together in a 1968 race, less than a mile to the finish. Said Walsh, "My coach told me, 'When Perrina fades, run like hell!'" Perrina weakened, Walsh got on his horse and won by 50 yards. Perrina faded to sixth, 100 yards off the pace.

5. CONTACT FEET

In track, you face disqualification if you impede the progress of another runner. In road running, the tenor is good-natured. In cross-country, you must be aggressive, and that means dishing it out and taking it.

You're on a narrow path, and there are two runners in front of you holding you back. There is no time for etiquette. You run through them. I've seen this happen many times on the final straightaway leading to the chute. A cluster of runners is worn to the core, blocking the direct path to the finish. Rushing behind them is a runner who saved a little. He's almost sprinting. What to do?

He plows through them. There may be several team points involved. Victory and defeat hang in the balance. Furthermore, in large fields where space is at a premium, shoulders will jar, legs will cross, elbows will flare and feet will meet. Since some runners wear spikes, getting spiked is a possibility.

6. SPACED OUT

Many US courses, especially those *not* on golf courses, are designed in such a way that there is a long, hilly portion sandwiched between the opening and closing flats. This is so because these routes go through parks, and it is important to start and finish in a wide-open area and also give the harriers a sufficient taste of the park's primal offerings.

Good field position is crucial in these instances. A runner who lags at the start will find it almost impossible to make up appreciable yardage in the thick of a crowd winding through the hills. Size is a factor. The taller and wider you are, the more serious the dilemma.

Kip Sirma of victorious Texas-El Paso was the last runner "out" at the start of the 1976 NCAA run. ("It takes me time to get warmed up," he said later.) But at 5'6" and 120 pounds, he was able to sneak through the congestion and finish 14th. He also had six miles to work at it and a flat, airy golf course conducive to shifting pace.

I saw a high school runner of five feet do this at Van Cortlandt Park a few times. He used his weight, or the lack of it, to his advantage and helped his team win the New York state championship. Getting desirable position requires a near-sprint at the start and some very quick glances to both sides. You don't wish to get hemmed in either, even if you're up front, as a triangular wedge is being formed.

7. WHAT GOES UP...

Is a pain in the butt for those who know less than you do about the principles of hill running. Most runners probably believe it is best to attack uphill, as though in testimony to your savagery and determination, and to let up on the downhill, in testimony to your finesse—and fear. This may work well for some. The converse also has its faithful.

Listen to Kenny Moore, world-class runner, quoted by Hal Higdon in *Runner's World*: "Don't reach the top of a hill exhausted. I'll give up five or 10 yards uphill to anyone and get twice that down the other side if I'm able to save enough energy to keep my knees up."

Jon Anderson, 1973 Boston Marathon runner says Moore "is the best downhill runner in the world."

Fine theory, but does it work? After the 1975 Eastern States high school meet, Luis Ostolozaga of New York, who finished second, had the following comment about Chris Hallinan of New Jersey, who finished first: "He took off on the downhills and I didn't." Hallinan won by 15 yards. Luis had set the course record one week earlier and lost his bid for an unbeaten season.

The consensus tells us to lean into the hill, maintaining pace and possibly breaking contact with nearby runners; and on the downhill not to lean backward to brace the shock but to lean fearlessly perpendicular to the ground...and let it fly. For the less adventurous, like myself, it might be more advantageous just to maintain momentum during the entire process—no let-up but no let-fly either.

8. FITS AND OUTFITS

Dress for the occasion. To explain at length about hot and cold, protection and comfort, cotton and nylon is like mommy giving the Ten Commandments to her little Johnny. Just use your head.

A few important reminders: a couple of thin layers work better than one bulky one; high socks (even up the calf) may prevent abrasions from debris, bushes and branches; gloves (thin, woolen ones or "work" gloves) are great warming agents, and, at a buck or two, can be tossed away during a race without much guilt.

Regarding footwear, the suggested ridged or waffle-soled training shoes put out by the major manufacturers can be used for racing. They also have comparable racing models for a lighter fit. The highly regarded New Balance—and they are good, I wear them—are more suited for road racing than cross-country because of only a thinly ridged bottom. Converse, generally associated with basketball, has come out with racing and training shoes for running, and in the ads they appear patterned after the popular durable, grooved-bottom models.

The question is: spikes or flats? Less experienced runners are sometimes uncomfortable with spikes. The "feel" takes getting used to. There is also the added expense, because spikes are not also worn for road running. Spiked shoes are advised when footing is bad—either because of a basically tough course or foul weather. Some runners bring an assortment of shoes to a cross-country race, not knowing exactly what conditions will prevail at race time.

9. GAMBLE, NOT GAMBOL

Go for broke, but don't play around. Use cross-country races to test your nerve and your wits. It is a thinking man's (and woman's) sport. There is always something to do, to anticipate, to watch out for. Set a fast pace. Be judicious—but not too judicious. In baseball, they tell *you* to play ball and not let the ball play you. Race the cross-country course, defy it. Don't let it run you. But this is not foolproof; gambling never is.

Tony Colon is a Manhattan College graduate and Puerto Rican Olympian in the 1500 meters. He is a gambler at heart and has raced many distances on tracks, roads and cross-country terrain. He is a likeable fellow and at last check was working as a grammar school teacher in the notorious South Bronx. I came across a 1969 clipping of mine that told of a Colon cross-country race, the fall before he was to lead the nation's scholastic outdoor milers with a 4:06 clocking. The story, for the *Long Island Press*, reads:

"Tony Colon of Power Memorial gambled yesterday. It paid off—for Archbishop Molloy High School.

"Colon, competing in the Iona College Interscholastic Cross-Country Run at Van Cortlandt Park, went out 'too fast' in an effort to stay with the favorite, Denis Fikes, who went on to capture the seeded varsity title in 12:56.3.

"'I gambled in this first meet,' said Colon, 'to try and stay with Fikes.' As a result, Colon, usually a strong finisher, tired during the downhill portion of the 2-1/2-mile race and finished seventh. This caused Power to lose the team title to Molloy..."

Even though I suggested earlier that following an excessively hard pace is irrational, I admire the spirited Colon for his spunk. He tested himself and learned a valuable lesson.

10. GOOD TIMES AND BAD

Time and place are our main performance gauges. A myriad of factors influences them. When time falters, place can still be a source of pride and vice versa. In cross-country, time is of little value. Courses are not standardized, the "measured" distances are sometimes unreliable. This enables the runner to hide a bit—from others if not from himself—for what does a 26:18 on a "moderately hilly" 4.5-mile course really mean? (Nine minutes for two miles on the track—that has significance.) Especially when "I couldn't even move near that damn bridge," placing 20th in a field of 100 means something—depending on whether you had hoped to finish first or 51st.

Is there any way to judge time accurately? There are some very imperfect methods. You must know pace per mile, and you do not need a pocket calculator to compute the above example. A 26:18 for 4.5 miles computes to 5:44 per mile. If you can go under 31 minutes (about five-minute mile pace) for 10,000 meters on the road or track, that 5:44 tempo is not very good unless the many variables such as weather and course conditions were severe.

If you race a course without the historical perspective of New York's Van Cortlandt Park or California's Mt. SAC, remember first that five minutes per mile is the generally accepted pace for outstanding cross-country running. For 5000 meters (3.1 miles), a time of 15:30 or so is exceptional.

High school runners sometimes have an opportunity for time comparisons because of a phenomenon known as postal competition. Coaches from distant towns who meet at a clinic or a cocktail party may decide to have their cross-country teams compete against one another the following fall. On the same day, each coach races his runners the same distance, usually two or three miles, on a standard quarter-mile track. The times are tallied and compared. Coaches are on their honor to be fair and accurate.

There is also a popular national postal competition sponsored by the United States Track & Field Federation and *Track & Field News*. For example, a runner who has been achieving 16:00 times (5:20 mile pace) on not-so-tough three-mile cross-country circuits and throws in a 15-minute three-mile track postal, learns there is something that is not working properly out on the countryside.

York High of Elmhurst, Ill., won the national postal titles in the three-mile in 1975 and '76. In 1975, York averaged 14:40 (setting the record) for its five men. In 1976, the average was 14:53. Let's see how York did in three-mile cross-country.

In the 1975 state meet (a relatively flat route), the quintet averaged 14:53 (placing second); in 1976, the average was 14:56 (placing third). Theoretically, this implies that York had a bit more to give in cross-country in 1975. And that bears out because York went into the state finals as the team favorite and came out with a surprise four-point loss.

Admittedly, this is patchwork figuring at best. Yet it serves to point out that cross-country times are not always insignificant. Use your personal barometer to assess them.

So what is our magic formula?

"Running well in cross-country," advises Western Kentucky coach Del Hessel, "requires one to remember that there is always something to *do* at all times. One should always be trying to catch someone, maintain the pace or prevent someone from catching up. Turns, hills and narrow passages constantly pull the pace down. Competitive concentration for an effort of long duration will produce a successful race."

Coaches often speculate about the relationship between fall cross-country and spring track success. Does the distance runner who treats cross-country with dedication stand a better chance of track reward than one who takes the fall sport lightly, all other things being equal? We are still waiting for the definitive scientific study. Here is a statistical sampling, using the finish of the NCAA 10,000 meter cross-country championship in Denton, Tex., in November 1976 and the NCAA 10,000-meter track race in Champaign, Ill., in June 1977. It should be noted that the cross-country course in Denton was mostly flat and therefore fast.

TRACK, CROSS-COUNTRY COMPARISON

NCAA TRACK 10,000 (6/77)			NCAA X-C (11/76)	
1. Kimombwa, Wash. St.	28:10.3		2.	28:16
2. Virgin, Illinois	28:22.5		3.	28:26
3. Sirma, Texas-El Paso	28:35.2		15.	29:00
4. Alitz, Army	28:36.8		27.	29:16
5. Treacy, Providence	28:41.4		5.	28:34
9. Kenny, E. Tenn. St.	29:21.3		37.	29:25
10. Rono, Wash. St.	29:22.6		1.	28:06
11. Richardson, MIT	29:39.8		140.	30:20
12. Shoots, Arizona	29:41.4		85.	29:56
13. Chapa, Oregon	29:42.4		9.	28:49
15. Pfitzinger, Cornell	29:45.1		132.	30:16
16. Braille, Bucknell	29:53.8		247.	31:36
17. Buell, Kentucky	30:01.2		138.	30:19
18. Garcia, Texas-El Paso	30:02.9		52.	29:42
19. Sonnenfeldt, Tenn.	30:04.4		86.	29:56
23. Stintzi, Wisconsin	30:19.8		102.	30:03
25. Redhair, Brigham Young	30:24.6		17.	29:03
26. Taylor, Rutgers	30:24.9		65.	29:48
29. Avery, Illinois	30:43.3		73.	29:50
31. Callaghan, St. John's	31:38.7		223.	31:10
32. Needler, Ball State	32:01.1		124.	30:13
35. Maritim, Texas-El Paso	DNF		8.	28:46
36. Slaughter, Tennessee	DNF		183.	30:44
37. Vega, Tennessee	DNF		163.	30:32
38. Zuniga, Texas-El Paso	DNF		181.	30:43

DNF—Did not finish

Of the 21 runners who finished both events, 11 ran faster in the cross-country race. This would seem remarkable except for the fact that weather conditions were extremely important here, and the weather in Denton was a perfect blend of sun and chill. Since 322 runners started the cross-country race and only 38 started the track event, place analysis is also without too much foundation.

A point could be made about cross-country victor Henry Rono placing 10th on the track, 100 yards ahead of Frank Richardson, 140th in cross-country and about a half-mile behind Rono. But then we would have to dissect the entire competitive year for Rono and Richardson to draw any conclusions of merit. Thus, I offer this chart merely as an appetizer. Let the researchers do something with it.

14
Organizing

"Hey, he cut the course!"
"It's pouring. Should we run?"
"Sorry, Coach, we took a wrong turn."
"You didn't score my fourth man."
"I didn't know freshmen could run."
"Whaddaya mean my entry wasn't in on time?"
"Who was 69th? He had no card."
"Where are the results already? Our bus is ready to go."
"What record? I missed it by only one second?"
"No one told us about the hills."

These outcries are music to a meet director's ears—bad music. They are vibrations of confusion, conflict and controversy, not exactly the hallmark of a successful cross-country meet. Win, lose or draw, cross-country should be a satisfying experience. But when the above comments hit like a machine gun fire, it becomes evident that many persons involved did not have a good time. In fact, some things may have been downright unfair.

The task of conducting a successful cross-country meet is formidable; indeed, it is challenging. If you are not patient, humble, efficient, determined, sensitive, clever, authoritative, demanding, ambitious... enough already, let's say a saint, don't apply for the job. Yes, it's tough.

So the first morsel of advice is: if you haven't been around, if you haven't seen your share of meets from the ground up, and haven't yet gained a good deal of experience and forethought, run for President of the United States or become a world-class marathoner. That's easier.

But the intent here is not to be discouraging. As we'll find out in this chapter, there is more than meets the eye. The neophyte should not jump into something he will regret.

Track meets also can be a demanding endeavor, but for them there is the welcome homogenity that does not exist for cross-country. Generally, quarter-mile (or 400-meter) tracks are used. And the program of events is somewhat basic, from the 100-yard dash to the distances and relays to the field events.

Cross-country is very diverse (which is something that disturbs a number of track fans, who dwell upon conformity and comparative performance). The conditions can differ greatly from one meet to another. Still, a set of guidelines can be established and adapted to meets of varying sizes and shapes.

The sizes of meets—the main factor in how a meet will be administered—fall into such categories as small (dual meet or just a handful of teams), medium (perhaps 10-20 teams), large (21-50 teams) and extra large (more than 50). Just like T-shirt sizes. And T-shirts can add a nice touch to a meet—more on that later.

These designations are arbitrary, but they are intended to represent a typical region of the country in terms of both general population and running population. The extremes are, well, extreme. There are the armies of participants in the New York City and Southern California areas. There are the small clusters of activity that dot the rural farmlands and mountain locales. This is true for almost any sport. If an average New York meet were picked up and dropped on Montana, they would have to call out the National Guard just to do the scoring.

The points that follow are made with a medium-sized meet in mind, one that is quite a bit larger than a dual but perhaps not as inflated as the scene at New York's Van Cortlandt Park on a fall Saturday. Still, some suggestions will be tailored also to encompass the extremes.

There is no substitute for advance planning. Every conceivable situation must be anticipated, and preventive and/or corrective measures must be decided upon as insurance should these situations arise.

Months before the day of the meet, scores of details must be ironed out, and as the meet nears, the subtleties must be isolated and finessed. All margin for error must be reduced as much as possible, if not entirely erased.

All the "What ifs...?" must be tackled before the meet, not when they occur. Then, it may be too late. Those who have managed cross-country meets know there is probably more work to be done prior to the meet that during and after one. Alright, now let us be specific.

CROSS-COUNTRY CHECKLIST

1. Need. Does your area really need another meet? If so, proceed diligently. But make sure first. There may already exist a burgeoning program. Maybe there are too many meets already. Another meet may detract from the established events that have acquired longtime respect and attention.

Why diffuse or congest a calendar of proper proportion? Too much of anything, even cross-country, is not good. If your intention is to go head-to-head with other competition, fine, but are you really helping cross-country or catering to your ego. Soul-searching is among the first priorities.

2. Scope. Are you thinking high school or college, or both? It must also be decided whether there will be "open" competition, or Masters, age-group or other special races, even a coaches' race. Is this a varsity-type meet, or will all grades and classes get a chance?

3. Level. Some runners run a lot faster than others. Some teams are much better than others. What are you going after—the elite or the rank-and-file, or a combination of both? If you are interested in a high-level meet, there comes with it additional responsibilities that may not exist for an event of lesser repute.

For example, a seeding committee may be required to establish an equitable race alignment. Also, courses that are suited to average runners may not be suited to the exceptional runners, who tend to remain in groups for a longer distance before "thinning out." Moreover, a chute mishap or scoring error might be considered more critical by championship-caliber teams than by coaches who are "building character," not trophy rooms.

4. Size. The principles involved in the management of a meet are almost the same for events small and large. Large meets simply magnify what has to be done. For small-scale activity, the size can be pre-determined by a coaches' agreement. If five coaches get together and decide to run a meet, everything is simplified, and the size of the field can be figured perhaps to the exact number of participants.

Sometimes, coaches are more ambitious. They become promoters and entrepreneurs and, incredibly enough, they pull it off. It is now common to find meets with more than 1000 athletes divided into separate divisions.

The size of a meet should be considered carefully, for it will affect every other consideration, from crowd control to parking to prizes to scoring procedures.

5. Site. There is usually little choice. If there are several available courses, it is because they are needed to service large populations and, in turn, their frenetic running activities. Some small towns have one sizable spot. In either case, it may be a take-it-or-leave-it situation. A spacious grass-and-dirt surface is nice, and that is most likely to be found in a park, on a golf course or on school grounds. The site could be restrictive and may prevent you from developing your meet into a grand affair.

Then, again, the facilities could be more than you had ever hoped for, enabling, for example, an awards ceremony and post-race buffet. The site must at least have the minimum requirements for health and safety, and be accessible to the teams that will be participating.

Permission must be obtained to use certain sites. This might entail a letter from a college president allowing you to use his golf course or an official permit from a police department allowing you to use a municipal park. If you are interested in a popular site, be sure that when you stake your claim at 9 a.m. on a Saturday, someone else is not already there with a briefcase full of documents proving he applied for the site before you.

6. Course. At many sites, there are standard courses that have been in use for years. Just make sure debris (like a fallen tree) has not made the route too hazardous, that it is clearly marked and has been measured accurately. A three-mile course should be just that—not 3.12 miles, for then frowned-upon timing discrepancies will be apparent and you will incur the wrath of school authorities for violating the maximum race-distance rules.

If you run into the problem of plotting a new course, there are many factors to keep in mind. There must be markers at every half-mile or mile point to indicate the distance traveled. The route must be easy to follow, preferably one big loop. A chalked line can mark the start. Flags or signs can mark the path.

The course must be challenging enough to test the better runners but not so difficult as to force weaker harriers to stop or drop out. It must be wide enough to enable large clusters of runners to pass most sections without incident. It should put the field into occasional view of spectators. It should be particularly wide down the homestretch so that a mad run-for-the-wire dash would not be throttled. The finish should flow easily into the chute (more on chutes later), and there should be enough room for workers to work, coaches to coach and athletes to embrace.

Purists (like myself) may wish to conduct cross-country in its most natural form with obstacles left or placed purposely along the route. There are many available options. A hill that is very steep or very long could be used. Sandy stretches and small patches of water—like the bunkers and water hazards of golf courses—can add a novel touch to a race. Then, there is the classic barrier similar to a steeplechase hurdle that will add a European flavor to the run, not to mention its quality as a lure for photographers.

At their worst, these touches can be dangerous. But some folks feel that is what cross-country is all about: man against the elements. At their best, they will make a meet more of an attraction. It must always be kept in mind that difficult courses are for experienced talents, not for the newcomers who are just getting used to the sport.

7. Date. The best date is one that is open. It is the dream of all young meet directors: The Open Date. Probably in 1977, there is no such thing because, happily, cross-country is growing to sizable proportions. Weekdays are usually bad because dual meets—to which schools are bound by league rules—are held. It is also difficult to get a large crew of workers to commit itself to a Wednesday. We are a nation of Saturdays.

League rules specify the opening and closing dates in which competition can be entered. Your best bet is to consider an early-season meet, since from mid-season on many teams are tied up with state qualifying and championship events. Early in the year, coaches look for alternative events that will enable their teams to gain experience without the pressures of must-win situations.

The weather must not be ignored. In the North, late-season races have been hit by snow. In the South, early-season races have been stifled by the heat.

League rules are also clogged with minimums and maximums—the minimum amount of time that must pass between meets, the maximum number of meets that can be run in one week, etc.

162

In addition to convenience, Saturdays are ripe because it increases your chances of media coverage. Part-time reporters put in time on Saturdays, and the Sunday sports section is the roomiest of the week. In towns that do not see a Sunday edition, newspapers tend to assemble a large Monday "wrapup" of the weekend's events. Negatively speaking, Saturday meets buck football for space in the Sunday paper. And in that contest, cross-country is the definite loser. (Media relations coming up soon.)

8. Sanctions. This has little relevance on the college level where schedules are frequently planned a year in advance. The athletic departments function as the sanctioning bodies, and the host institution bears the responsibility of meet conduct.

For high schools, a carefully specified procedure must be adhered to for interstate contests. Applications for sanction must be submitted in accordance with state rules to the National Federation of State High School Athletic Associations (P.O. Box 98, Federation Place, Elgin, Ill. 60120). A request must be made for each state from which a team's entry is anticipated.

Individual states also have their own guidelines. And sometimes there are also sanctioning procedures for intrastate events where there exists a segmented administration consisting of several autonomous associations.

For open competition, it may be advantageous to have AAU assistance and its allied sanctions.

9. Rules Application. Rules for competition vary from league to league and state to state. They include athletes' age, distance of race, time lapse between competition, mixed (male and female) events, etc. You must decide the set of rules under which the meet will operate. If team A wins the title, it is subsequently discovered that one of its runners turned 19 years old before Sept. 1, and your association considers him ineligible, imagine the outcries that will follow.

10. Entry Fees. Basically, the going rate should be good enough for you, too. A standard charge may be $5 or $10 per team (seven runners), depending on the number of teams expected, the number and quality of the awards, the need for additional personnel and the existence of any meet embellishments such as a free clinic or lunch.

11. Financial Support. The quality of your meet can be enhanced by an organization willing to underwrite the expenses in exchange for the advertising it will accrue by such promotion. The rules can be ticklish

163

here, since the main sponsoring body still must be a school, and not the slightest hint of any foul play with regard to the amateur bylaws should exist.

12. Race Setup. There is not only one way to do it. A small entry may enable a meet to put the entire field into one race of 100 or so harriers. The more runners, the more races. You have to determine the maximum number of teams that can run in a given race, and your main criteria for that must be caliber of running and safety. Also, will you set up your fields based on ability (varsity, junior varsity), age (seniors, juniors, sophs) or enrollment (large, medium, small schools)?

Be careful about the designations given to race. Runners do not like to be labeled negatively. Who does? When I ran cross-country, rather slowly, in the New York City high school program in the early 1960s, occasionally I was entered in a division called "scrub." I could have won and smashed a record, but to myself—and to my classmates and neighbors—I was still a "scrub." What a self-image!

It's hard to get out there every day and put in the mileage when you know that, come Saturday, to all the world you will be a scrub. The only imaginable benefit to this disparagement is that it might seem so punitive that a harrier would make a remarkable improvement just to escape this race classification. Still, would it be worth the embarrassment? More often than not, it would have a detrimental effect on his running interests.

Thankfully, the scrub race has left New York, and I have not come across it elsewhere. Everyone cannot run on the first-string varsity. For those who cannot, the cross-country experience is not necessarily diminished. But let's be fair. Euphemisms, in this case, are appropriate. All the races can be called "varsity," and they can be distinguished by Roman numerals (I, II, III, etc.) or letters (Varsity A, Varsity B, etc.), or even by being named after persons who have given devoted service to the sport (The John Smith Race, etc.)

There is an engaging approach to race organization that is used too sparingly. It is called "sweepstakes." Even the name is enticing. There are several types, but for every type the rationale is that there will be crowned one grand, or overall, champion from among the many races. A mild form merely takes the team with the fastest (five-man) time and finds it the titlist.

Better to do it this way: Run five (or seven) races. The first race will have the runners designated by their coaches as the team's seventh fastest men. The second race will have the sixth fastest, and so on, until

164

the final race, which will have in it the number-one harriers from each team. The scoring would be cumulative, and the team with the low aggregate total would be declared the sweepstakes champion. Awards should still be given in each division with a grand prize to the sweepstakes winner.

The excitement would be terrific. Theoretically, the slowest man would become as important as the stud. The weaker varsity members could place well and even have a chance to win, because they would be matched with counterparts of equal strengths. The tallies would take on a decathlon impact in that the team standings would fluctuate until the dramatic finale.

There would be the option of scoring a team's best five places—not the entire seven (if seven races were run)—to account for DNF's and other maladies. Otherwise, a mishap in the first race, for example, could kill the entire meet for a particular team.

This system is advisable for large invitationals in excess of 40 or 50 teams, since the number of teams entered would be the same number of runners in each division. Moreover, since this can be done for only one varsity unit, a meet using this setup would also be obliged to accommodate the teams' other runners with other races.

Colleges don't have such worries, because much of their program revolves around dual meets in which full teams compete in one race. Their teams number only 10-15 runners, and for larger invitationals there might be a "junior" or "B" division for second-string units.

13. Awards. It is always nice when every runner can go home with something. Even if it is a certificate of minimal expense that merely states, "Joe Runner has successfully completed the Middletown Cross-Country Invitational . . ."—it will be valued by the recipient.

Beyond that, trophies, plaques, medals, ribbons and T-shirts—the standard prize fare—should be awarded equitably and generously when possible. Take into account the caliber of the competitors, the significance of the meet, and revenues realized from entry fees, program advertising or commercial sponsorship.

At the very least, 25% of all participants should receive some sort of an award. Consult the catalogs for the best prices. Discounts for bulk orders are available. If, say, 150 prizes were awarded at a meet involving 500 athletes, the entry revenue (at $1.00 or so per competitor) would pay for the entire package. Order early; don't trust the post office to save you. One meet director in the East orders his prizes for the following year about 10 months in advance so he can beat the inevitable cost increase caused by inflation.

Incidentally, reading matter makes for fine awards. Running publications can be obtained in large quantities at discount rates. Publishers are always anxious to attract new subscribers.

14. The Entry Blank. Take the basic 8-1/2 x 11-inch sheet of blank white paper and fill up both sides with every bit of information pertinent to the meet. Include: name, date, site, course, distance, time schedule, race setup, entry limitations, entry fee, prize structure, entry deadline, travel directions, overnight accommodations, rules in use, sanctioning bodies, dressing facilities, etc. Have a section for information about the school (address, coach's name, phone, enrollment). Have a spot for the principal's signature, which should legally "waive" all meet sponsors and officials of any claim made by an injured runner.

One sheet is usually enough. Coaches can easily make a few copies via school photostat machinery. For a clean finish, have the entry blank printed professionally through the offset method. (One thousand copies may cost about $20). Mimeographed reproduction is sometimes sloppy. An additional page could be used for a course map, especially if there is a large out-of-town entry.

All of the information must be clear. Ambiguities can haunt you come post time. For example, will it be your policy to return the entry fee to a school that did not show up? If the weather is horrendous, could there be a possible postponement or cancellation?

15. Crowd Control. Alright, stop laughing. Sure, who shows up at a cross-country meet besides the athletes and coaches? First of all, even *they* are part of the "Crowd"—or all of it, as the case may be. You can't have hundreds (or thousands) of runners just everywhere, and what about coaches, moms and dads, and the ice cream vendors?

Crowd control for cross-country means making sure there is no interference along the racing course and at the chute, and no intrusion at any outdoor installation used for scoring, officiating, awards pickup, the press or medical care. This is not so easy.

There are sites at which crowds converge on the course, creating a narrow funnel for oncoming runners. How unfair! The funnel effect is even more contemptible down the homestretch when last-gasp kicks bring runners to the chute four abreast. It is wise to designate spectator, or viewing, areas with flags or signs, especially when the route is a sprawling golf course. The aforementioned outdoor installations should be roped off or guarded. Imagine the intricacies of scoring upset by impatient coaches pleading for immediate results.

Some people are difficult to contain with standard crowd-control measures. Like rugby players, as noted earlier. The 1975 IC4A meet was held up when stubborn rugby players refused to clear the starting area, which crossed their turf. They finally acquiesced, but not before a few punches were thrown (by them).

Bullhorns or a full-fledged public address system is invaluable in alerting onlookers to the whereabouts of the racers. They are also useful in gathering the athletes to the start, awarding prizes, giving color commentary of the race, stating background information about the leading competitors, promoting future events, generating enthusiasm, hailing meet sponsors and workers, calling for a doctor and finding the mother of a lost child.

Two-way radios can be used indirectly as a crowd-control measure. By reporting the progress and pace of a race, you keep spectators alerted and develop a rapport with the audience. This is particularly welcome when most of the course is beyond the view of the crowd. People without stopwatches can lose track of time and inadvertently mill around on parts of the course.

We hear a lot about crowd-control for sports events, but for basketball, football and the like, the element of control is inherent in the activity. There are specific seats and the game transpires right in front of you. Cross-country meanders all over the place, often in conflict with other events at the same general site. Be careful.

16. Officials. A meet director is tantamount to an executive in private industry. He must be able to attract and evaluate ample personnel and delegate authority with sense and candor. He forms a staff of competent workers. Here is a list of all possible positions that could be required to conduct a successful meet. When necessary, job descriptions also are listed. (Obviously, small meets do not need *all* of these people.)

1. Meet Director
2. Assistant Meet Director.
3. Referee.
   (These three form the Meet Committee that will rule on infractions, protests, etc.).
4. Starter.
5. Starting Line Clerks.
6. Timers.
7. Place Recorders.
8. Chute Crew.

9. Runners (who transport finish cards and other scoring data from chute to scorers).

10. Scoring Crew (includes several people to assort place cards, tabulate results, type, call of names or numbers, mimeograph, depending on the system in use).

11. Awards Custodian.

12. Inspectors (out on the course to direct the athletes, control crowds, monitor course cutting or rules infractions).

13. Doctor and/or Trainer.

14. Announcer.

15. Equipment Custodian (to transport, set up and put back chute apparatus, benches, tables, flags, markers, etc., to clean up).

16. Program Committee (just a typist or two or several persons involved in advertising, production, printing, statistics, depending on the "program" in use).

17. Meet Photographer.

18. Press Liaison (to send out advance publicity releases to the press, arrange for interviews, distribution of results).

19. Video Crew (if video will back up scoring should a manual error occur).

20. Tape Recorder (if tape will back up scoring should a manual error occur).

21. Food Committee (to see or distribute refreshments).

22. Social Committee (to accommodate overnighters, arrange for pre-meet festivities and/or post-meet awards or buffet...to charm dignitaries)

23. Security (Local police—just their presence is always helpful as a deterrent to potential rowdies).

24. Singer or Recording (of the National Anthem).

25. Marshalls (euphemism for people there when you need them for miscellaneous duties, should, for example, crowd control get sticky or weather become nasty).

For a major invitational or championship meet with all the trimmings, as many as 50 persons can be required to handle all of the assignments. The smaller the meet, the fewer the personnel.

Even though these people may be dedicated saints who revel in cross-country company, they are entitled to something more than a morning cup of coffee, a T-shirt and a pat on the back. At the very least, a hearty lunch should be served them. More properly, they should be paid—from $10 to $25 (and up). This becomes quite a payroll when 50 officials are involved, but any meet requiring 50 officials would be bringing in a tidy sum from entry fees. Treat your helpers well. You want them back next year.

17. Scoring. In cross-country, you win by having fewer. This is another unique aspect to the sport; the team with the fewest points wins. The basic rule is simple: a team gets the exact number of points of the places its runners attain for the race. The victorious runner scores one point for its team, the second-place runner scores two points and so on. The only exception to this occurs when the displacement method is used, and even then the principles remain the same. Displacement will be explained shortly.

In most cross-country meets in the United States, a team's total score is compiled by adding the places of the first five runners from its unit who complete the race. Thus, a team would score 168 points if its runners place third, 10th, 34th, 40th and 81st.

Schools generally run between five and seven runners. Even though the sixth and seventh men to finish do not score, their places serve to add points for other teams, thereby enhancing their own chances of team success.

Sometimes, for dual meets, opposing coaches may wish to run almost their entire squads—15 runners or more from each side—and agree to do so. The same scoring principle will still be used, with only each team's first seven runners figured in the tabulation.

Incidentally, if fewer than five runners finish a race, the team is automatically disqualified. That is why most teams take advantage of the rules and run six or seven runners as permitted.

(In the 1975 and '76 NCAA Championships Washington State, serious contenders, gambled and brought only five men to the starting line. A lost shoe, a spiked heel, an upset stomach—whatever—would have disqualified coach John Chaplin's harriers. But bad luck did not intrude, and State placed second and third, respectively, in the standings.)

Ties can occur in cross-country, but there are no extra innings or sudden-death periods. In fact, there is not even one generally accepted way to break the tie. Ties can come about in dual meets (the score would be 28-28) and in larger meets where teams can tie for first place or any other position. The NCAA rules are quite clear: in case of a tie, score only the first four runners from each team; if a tie still exists, score only the first three. These rules are clear, but they would not win a popularity contest at a coaches' convention.

In 1976, *The Harrier* editorialized, "The way you break ties should combine your philosophy about cross-country as a sport with the practicality of the circumstances at hand. In the high school sphere, there are all sorts of methods, depending on state rules, agreements by opposing coaches, league differences, etc. Some use the higher finish of a team's first man. Some use the higher finish of a team's fourth, fifth or sixth man. Some add up the performances and match the aggregate times to break the tie.

"The NCAA four-man rule reduces the emphasis that might be given to a varsity's sixth and seventh men. Some coaches may only run five men for that reason, gambling that a DNF will not occur. Using the lead man as a tiebreaker is foolish, especially in large meets, because it undermines the team concept.

"We prefer the sixth-man adaptation because of the stimulating effect it might have on the slower runners of a team's varsity. Imagine a guy (or gal) who never won anything given a hero's welcome at the finish for giving 100% and enabling his team to win an all-important meet by one point."

In response to that viewpoint, Rich Stevens, cross-country coach at Marist College, Poughkeepsie, N.Y., wrote, "I feel that cross-country ties should always be decided by the same method and should not be left to the discretion of meet directors or coaches 'after the fact.' I am not pleased with the method of breaking ties (NCAA rule: score the first four men) that now exists, since cross-country is defined as a five-man sport. The scores of five men are supposed to count.

"Therefore, I advocate that in an invitational, if a tie exists between two teams, then check the score of the two teams as if they had met in a dual meet to determine the victor (or better place)....This proposal could be extended to apply to a tie among three or more teams."

Although the actual scoring is done after the race, the scoring mechanisms are activated prior to the competition. The procedures in use will determine the kinds of numbers worn by the runners, the coaches' responsibilities, the formation and control of the chute, and how many people complain they were railroaded. The options run the gamut of simple to complex.

In the vast majority of races, there is "straight" scoring. Every runner entered is a member of a competing team. No one is participating individually. In those rare events—mainly some of the national meets—when teams *and* individuals vie in the same event, the displacement method is used. Here, the places of individuals not on teams are discarded in the team scoring; that is, they are displaced. That is why a team can score under 200 points without having a runner in the top 50 finishers.

Let us examine a few of the alternatives in ordinary, straight (no displacement) team scoring. Give each coach index cards—the kind with the hole in them—for his runners. The athlete's name and team

170

are written on it, preferably with a felt-tip pen that will resist moisture.

When the runner enters the chute, a marshall snatches off his card and collects them in sets of 50 or 100 and puts a rubber band around them. (Blank cards must be available for officials to quickly jot down the name and school of a finisher whose card was lost in transit.) An official takes the sets to the scoring table.

As the cards are numbered, the teams are called off and the scores are placed on a large cardboard-like sheet. The figures are tabulated—and there you are. After the team tally has been completed, a typist can prepare the individual results (after also getting the timers' sheet) and the team standings on the same stencil for subsequent duplicating.

As a backup in case of error, an inspector can patrol the chute and call off numbers in order into a small cassette recorder. This is only possible if runners have been given specified numbers—not if the "card-snatch" method is in use. If the runners have indeed been given printed numbers, the numbers should be grouped consecutively by team.

In a moderately sized meet, officials can call out the numbers of the finishing runners; one calls and another writes them down. However, this procedure is susceptible to error because of bunching at the finish. When a half-dozen harriers charge the chute, it is perhaps physically impossible—if other runners are soon to follow—to distinguish the numbers, call them off and write them down without error.

I suppose it can be done if aggressive inspectors are standing by to separate and move the traffic at the mouth of the chute. Then, a recording error can be corrected. Or the recording of numbers can be done less hectically if the officials wait until the runners have entered the chute and their movement has stopped. The field will have to be contained in order in the chute, enduring discomfort for many minutes while the tally is made. Chute personnel must be sensitive yet firm in maintaining decorum and efficiency.

For the ultimate in precaution, the system of two-part numbers and videotape backup used in collegiate championships is advisable. The video setup is not as extravagant as it appears. Almost every high school and certainly every college has such equipment for use in the classroom. Set up the video on a platform overlooking the finish line, and tape the entire field as it enters. A slow-motion device will help officials confirm the placing after the race.

Regarding the two-part numbers, the NCAA handbook states:

Prepared perforated cards with the runner's name, assigned number, school and graduating class should be stapled at the base of the *cloth* number to be worn on the front (sic) chest. Included in both halves of the card should be a large space for an official to mark the finish place of each runner.

"The lower half of the perforated card will be collected by officials as the runners leave the chute out the far end.... The upper half of the perforated card, left on the runner's number, must be collected by the runner's coach, placed in the quick-score envelope furnished for this purpose and returned to officials in the quick-score area. The place marked on the perforated card indicates the official position of the runner... confirmed by the referee after he observes the official films.

In the less elaborate snatch-card method, coaches also are able to compile a quick score and serve as a safeguard against scoring malfunction. Numbers are marked on small strips of paper (or cardboard) and given by officials to runners in the chute. The winner gets number one and so on. The runner gives his number to his coach, who writes it down on a form provided him and submits it to the referee. Any discrepancies can be ironed out unless a runner, wiped out by the stress of the race, loses the numbered card.

It is imperative that the chute be designed to accommodate as many runners as possible and to also enable efficient management by officials. The mouth of the chute should be at least 10 feet wide. The actual funnel should be about three feet in width. There is a formula for length that requires at least one foot per runner—100 feet of chute length for 100 harriers.

One can use a single chute or a double chute (or even a triple one). As the name implies, the single chute has one roped-off path through which the finishers will run. The double chute has two sections, one of which is closed at all times so that the harriers will not funnel into the wrong one.

The second part is needed in case the first one clogs up (in large races); thus, runners simply filter into the open pathway. The chutes are then used alternately, as each becomes vacant. The idea is to move the runners quickly, avoiding a jamup and completing the scoring tasks accurately. Marshalls must be assertive in directing the onrushing finishers to the proper chute, assuring the correct order in the chute and "pushing" the fatigued competitors out of the chute to make room for following harriers.

A foulup in the chute at the 1973 IC4A meet in New York City caused the contestants to back up out the mouth of the chute and onto the racing course. More than a few runners were shaken up by the

EXAMPLES OF FINISH LINE CHUTE MANAGEMENT

Diagram of Single Chute

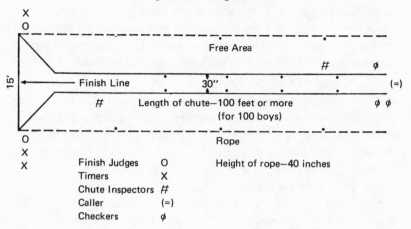

Finish Judges   O   Height of rope—40 inches
Timers   X
Chute Inspectors   #
Caller   (=)
Checkers   φ

Diagram of Double Chute

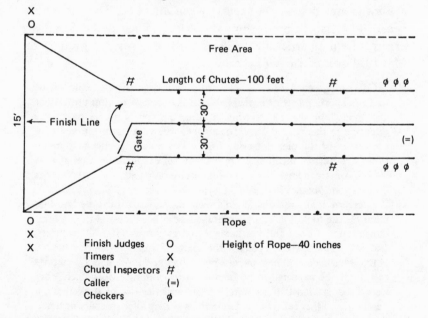

Finish Judges   O   Height of Rope—40 inches
Timers   X
Chute Inspectors   #
Caller   (=)
Checkers   φ

Source: 1977 handbook of the National Federation of State High School Athletic Associations, Clifford B. Fagan, publications editor and executive secretary.

173

chain reaction of bumping shoulders as incoming competitors could not hit their brakes in time and slammed into the waiting, chilled finishers.

Officials panicked. They manhandled some of the athletes in an attempt to avoid chaos. Finally, the whole mess was sorted out, and the team scores were said to have been accurate. Still, the exact places of some runners in the back of the pack were never determined.

18. Publicity. There are two kinds of reporters who cover cross-country: the ones that want to be there and the ones that do not. The former category applies to journalists who have long endured the lack of amenities at cross-country meets and will succeed in spite of handicaps in covering the events and getting their stories through the appropriate channels. Like the finer athletes, they thrive on adversity.

The latter group would rather be at the local football game—or perhaps anywhere else—than "wasting time" chasing after heaving runners at a rain-driven park. They would rather be enjoying the comforts of a stadium press box—although some of them are hardly comfortable, take my word for it—watching end runs and halter tops through spyglasses.

Both groups deserve your courtesy and attention. There is mutual benefit to a smooth press connection. How do you do it? Below are excerpts from an article ("Our Piece of the Publicity") I wrote in the May 1974 issue of *Runner's World:*

> Competitive road running and cross-country is the stepchild of the nation's sports pages. Preoccupied with the money-making professions and guided by our ball-playing culture, the sports media pays little attention to the runner. Sure, track races receive a share—however inadequate—of the pie. But aside from a few events, particularly marathons like Boston, it can be estimated without exaggeration that at least 90% of American long-distance races receive only token (if any) coverage by the sports press.
>
> There are many reasons for this vacuum. Perhaps it can be said that money is the root of all sports coverage—or at least most of it. Get some movie star to start a golf tournament and give away $100,000 in prizes, and he'll be guaranteed a place in the hearts of American sports editors.
>
> Decision-makers at newspapers, magazines and radio and TV stations can hardly be expected to be familiar with running. Most likely, they were bred (as most of us were) on an athletic diet of basketball or baseball, and they reflect that diet in the way they allocate space or time.
>
> In general, the print media has suffered from a decrease in advertising revenue. (The paper shortage hasn't helped either.) Less advertising (or paper) means a thinner newspaper. And when sports space tightens, don't expect the Super Bowl to be trimmed. Running also has felt the

effects of the enormous expansion of the professional ranks. With more leagues and more teams every year—and no end in sight—running coverage would seem to be headed for greater drought.

Alas, we cannot blame this unfortunate situation only on the sports editor, who is constantly pressured by lobbyists from various sports and publicists from various teams seeking equal space. The persons who conduct the running events—the directors or promoters—must share some of the blame.

The following suggestions are intended to help race directors gain more benefit from their local media. Obviously, there are differences among the media, and many of these points could be tailored appropriately.

BEFORE THE RACE.

1. Have you, well in advance of the race, formulated a list of the media that might be interested in your event?

2. Have you decided upon ways to keep them informed of race developments in the weeks preceding the race?

3. Have you sent pre-race notices that would include: expected number of participants; expected age range; whether women will compete with men; the number of races; a tentative time schedule; any course records and other pertinent statistics; a course layout (essential for TV camera crews and photographers)?

4. If possible, have you decided to hold your race early in the day so that reporters will have sufficient time to conduct interviews, obtain results and report the race fully and accurately?

5. Have you kept them informed of the entry of any "name" runner or local hero whose participation may require special coverage?

6. Have you, perhaps, organized a press luncheon in which reporters can mingle with (and interview) leading entrants, and photographers can accumulate photos? (This can serve as a press conference as well so that late meet changes can be announced.)

7. Have you designed your entry blank so that any unusual circumstances involving a runner's participation could be ascertained and, in turn, provide the media with a fresh "angle" prior to the race?

8. Have you arranged for the use of duplicating equipment (or at least a typist) that will make race results available quickly?

9. Will you have a full-scale race program or at least a mimeographed list of entrants' names and other essential information?

10. If the site of the race may be unfamiliar to the press, have you notified them of the availability of phones that may enable them to call in their stories?

11. If you will be too busy with other matters, have you assigned an assistant to handle this work and serve as a sort of press liaison?

DURING THE RACE

1. Are there tables and chairs as part of a "press area" where reporters can work if they so choose?

2. If a trail car is to accompany the field, is there room available for the press?

3. Is there is specific spot to which the winner will go after the race so that—when he is ready—he can be interviewed and photographed?

4. If there are several races, will results be distributed between races?

AFTER THE RACE

1. If press representation is weak, will someone phone in the highlights of the race to those reporters who did not attend?

2. Will official results be distributed as quickly as possible?

3. Have the dates of other (upcoming) races been announced?

The reporter, of course, assumes the responsibility of covering a race properly. But his unfamiliarity with the sport may not give him an inclination to even concern himself with running. Therefore, an event must be clarified for him so that he could recognize its importance and feel confident in the manner in which it could be covered.

19. Weather or Not. In some parts of the country, the weather is merely a gentle backdrop to the meet, hardly noticed amid consistently ideal running conditions. Elsewhere, there is a seasonal fluctuation—extreme heat or cold, persistent winds, periodic rain, even snow, or some nasty combination of all this. Sometimes, the weather seems so cruel, week after week, that it becomes almost endemic to the sport: what would cross-country be without a mini-hurricane?

Some of us may prefer it this way. We delight in coping with the elements, running in natural conditions under the fury of God. Or perhaps some of the time we are masochists. Psychologists like to say there is a little bit of masochism in all of us. And what better way to show it—as athlete, coach, spectator, reporter—than to soak up nature on a rainswept Saturday?

Whether or not we like raindrops falling on our heads, we had better prepare for the worst. No matter what the TV meteorologist tells you on Friday, be ready for anything on Saturday.

In October 1976, *The Harrier* reported: "The joke circulating around rain-whipped Van Cortlandt Park was that Manhattan College would have to put a dome over the 1200-acre Bronx site and conduct the world's first *indoor* cross-country meet.

"Amid storm conditions throughout the Northeast, the Weather Bureau in New York issued a 'Flood Watch,' a 'Tornado Watch' and a 'Gale Watch.' You could have watched it all at Van Cortlandt Park where 5000 runners fought the elements in the Manhattan College Interscholastic Cross-Country Meet.

"Plagued twice by rain in the previous three years, Manhattan officials, who had been working on the huge meet for months, resolutely completed the tasks required in sending off, managing and scoring 21 races in 15-minute intervals in what has become the nation's largest—and wettest—scholastic cross-country meet."

There are two lessons to be learned here:

First, miraculously, the races went off on time and 5000 runners cleared out of Van Cortlandt having done what they came for; diligent officiating paid off.

Second, the scoring was hardly a picture of perfection. The names and schools on the race cards worn by the runners were erased by the rain. Some cards became so crumpled by the wetness that they were lost along the race route, which resembled one long stream. The scoring was done by a half-dozen persons seated in the back of a rented truck. Because of the weather, many more persons, including awards personnel and reporters, sought shelter in this truck. Every time one of the doors would swing open, a splash of rain would sweep in. It was impossible to do all that paperwork and use a typewriter and mimeograph machine when everything was wet. Consequently, the scoring was much delayed and inaccurate in spots, and a few races were never figured out to anyone's satisfaction.

The officials could have worked in a nearby tavern or in Manhattan College itself, two indoor sites used in the past. But they wanted to be quick in awarding the prizes after the races went off. The solution would have been simple: Rent two or more trucks. Use one for awards, one only for scoring and others for miscellany (reporters, etc.) Use race cards of a heavier consistency, and give each coach a felt pen (which he can keep as a gift) to mark the cards. A meet with an entry of 5000 can afford the extra money for additional truck rental.

Really bad weather also yields this question: Should a cross-country meet ever be postponed because of adverse conditions? Before analyzing this, it should be noted that in a locale known for its poor weather, the policy of the meet should be clearly stated on the entry blank. Something to this effect: "Heavy snow, which is possible in November, would *not* postpone or cancel the meet. The race will go on no matter what."

Joe Fox, as coach and administrator, has probably done as much for track and cross-country in the New York City area as anyone. He is a prolific meet director, but it seems as though the rain just follows him around. In 1975, at the Eastern States Interscholastic Championships, sponsored by Fordham University, it rained so hard that the normally hazardous ups and downs at Van Cortlandt Park became more so, imperiling, in Joe's mind, the safety of the runners. Not everyone agreed with him.

"I'd rather have coaches yell at me," asserted Joe, the meet director, "than broken legs."

He had plenty of coaches yell at him, for they had traveled from Rochester and Philadelphia and other distant points, only to find the meet postponed—for five weeks—until the next available open date for most of the teams involved. Joe's decision was not rash or unilateral. He conferred with many coaches for a long time and personally surveyed the course during the downpour. Still, he caught hell. He could have avoided the negative reaction simply by having the meet's policy in bold letters on the entry blank, as mentioned earlier.

My own feeling is that there really can be no absolute rule. When the weather is extremely foul, and would possibly cause danger to the runners, consider: number of teams, importance of meet, out-of-town travel, future availability of site and date, etc. Opposing coaches can always agree about their dual meet. But a college conference or high school state meet is significantly diminished in the event of a postponement. All in all, I tend to sympathize with the idea that, no matter what, the show must go on.

20. Accommodations. Out-of-town schools may need a place to stay overnight. A school or YMCA may be available. Apply for discount rates at motels. Locker rooms and showers at the race site are always nice. Food vendors are a welcome amenity. Make sure the course is open for scouting and inspection prior to the meet for those unfamiliar with it.

21. Meetings. Officials' meetings should be held in advance of the meet for purposes of organization. If meetings are not possible until the night before, the officials should be notified by mail of the general meet operations and how their particular assignments fit in. For a large meet, don't expect merely to have all personnel show up an hour early and then figure the whole thing out.

22. Equipment. Make a list that includes everything but your toothbrush; don't forget anything. Ropes, bullhorns, stopwatches, starter's pistol, course markers, flags, pens and pencils, race cards, numbers, coaches' envelopes, programs and entry lists, typewriters, mimeograph machine (and stencils), safety pins, coffee urn (and coffee), etc. Have more than enough, and make sure your know who's bringing what.

23. Logistics. Now that you have remembered everything, where will you put it all? Where, for example, will the runners' sweatsuits be when they finish the race, if the start and finish are not in the same place? (And will it be the responsibility of the meet or the coaches to secure the team's belongings during the competition?)

24. Festivities. There are some meets that go the whole route. They have a night-before-the-meet dinner where a sumptuous buffet is polished off with enough beer to have drowned the allied forces in the last World War. Dignitaries from cross-country and other sports address the guests, and the next morning the local politicians show up to shoot the gun after pledging allegiance to a recording of the "Star Spangled Banner." Great—if you can set this up.

25. Sponsors. Money may be the root of all evil, but it can work wonders with an ailing cross-country meet. A prosperous business or other organization may be willing to exchange financial support for public relations gain. So what if you have to call your meet the "Smith Tool Company Cross-Country Run."

Having fun? Good, but you are not quite finished. Have a complete set of results printed with reproductions of newspaper coverage and other tidbits of information. Send copies to all coaches and ask for their feedback regarding the meet. Mention next year's date. Thank everyone for their cooperation. And get to bed early.

15
Watching

If your think cross-country racing requires special tactics, consider the spectators. Like hunters after their prey, they stalk the runners from one spot to the next, lining up their marks, dashing to key vantage points, trying to isolate their favorites. Having only minutes to view what they must, these determined onlookers go through a series of windsprints to catch up with the field while dressed in heavy garb and with running paraphernalia flying from every limb. No wonder the turnover rate is so high.

Some of the old reliables have given up. The veterans among them say they have not quit—but retired. The difficulties in watching cross-country are directly proportionate to the difficulties in running cross-country. Indeed, one must be fit, conditioned, in shape. When runners run hills, spectators run hills. When it rains on the runners, it pours on the spectators. Course routes have become more spread out, more intricate, more demanding, and meets have become larger and more complex. Spectators, too, must train and plan for cross-country. Watching the races is both an art and a science—a marvel when beautifully executed.

I have watched at least 200 cross-country meets during the last 15 years, and I am still not very good at it. That is mainly my own fault. I generally have so many responsibilities at a meet that I am unable to take the trouble or find the time to set up my viewing plans. Most of those responsibilities involve newspaper coverage, which has frequently precluded my enjoyment of the races but enable me to pay my phone bill.

As a reporter, I have had to station myself at the finish line—not so much to see the tape-breaking as to locate the winners and other runners for interviews germane to my stories. Sometimes, it is just not possible to absorb the heart of the race and also be there at the end with pen and pad, eagerly prepared to record the runners' revelations for tomorrow's editions and posterity. And even when I do find spare moment to drift into the woods, an acquaintance is bound to corner me with a monologue of cross-country trivia.

Most of my watching of cross-country has been at several sites in and around the New York metropolitan area and New York state's upper regions. I have also witnessed the action in Pennsylvania, Indiana, Maryland, Texas and Arizona while chasing after the national championships. A few of my out-of-town excursions have been quite memorable—for the wrong reasons, such as abominable travel conditions. But my Cross-Country-Lovers-Do-Anything-To-See-A-Meet Award goes not to myself but to my friend, Keith Markman, who has done a little running and a little coaching and a little of everything else in his salad days.

It was November 1972, and it was supposed to be the three of us—Keith, myself and Stuart Warner, marathon man and self-proclaimed know-it-all. We were to meet at Stu's house on Friday morning at 8 o'clock and drive 350 miles north to Rochester, site of the New York state meet the following day. Eight o'clock. No Keith. We waited and waited. Still, no Keith. Good-bye, Keith. This did not surprise us, knowing Keith's unpredictability.

It was 6 p.m., and Stu and I were having the traditional meet eve dinner of Holiday Inn magic, drowning our fatigue in running talk and general nonsense, and greeting coaches who arrived to do much of the same thing at nearby tables. At just about the time we had reached the skin of our baked potatoes and were lamenting Keith's absence, who do you suppose walked in nonchalantly with a knapsack on his back?

Right. Keith.

After oversleeping and finding us gone, he hitched beyond the maze of New York City's highways and all the way up the New York State

Thruway, a bitch of a road just to *drive* on. Stu and I were hysterical. Keith had spent the entire day thumbing rides, and what would he see the next day but a few fleeting glances of runners generally unfamiliar to him.

Keith is—still is—that kind of a guy. At running events all over the East, Keith is always the one who bunks on the floor of the motel room—for free—while a colleague and I split the room fare more comfortably. The last I heard, Keith was doing some teaching, some cab driving and some bartending. Warner, the third member on that Rochester trip, is a disciple of the Ayn Rand school of objectivist philosophy and is now a doctoral candidate at a Midwestern university.

As I said, my own race watching is amateur, but I must give myself a pat on the back for some keen juggling acts. One meet that comes to mind is the 1976 NCAA in Denton, Tex. I covered it for several publications, including three Eastern newspapers.

For the papers, I had to assure myself of capturing the "local angle," which meant watching and interviewing some middle-of-the-pack harriers from certain Eastern schools. For my own publication, I had planned to make the meet the lead story of my next issue with a 2500-word account full of race description, quotes and analysis. There were also deadlines to meet and a plane to catch.

Fortunately, the weather was excellent and the course was managable. I had a clipboard in my hand and an airlines bag weighing down my shoulder with a stopwatch, binoculars and other sundries. To see as much as I could, I traversed the route, a college golf course, from one mile marker to another, noting the procession of faces and numbers and medial times, and gauging the positions of contending teams.

At the last possible moment, I dashed to the finish, especially when it became clear that Henry Rono, the somewhat unknown African freshman from Washington State, would be the decisive winner. "Who is this guy, anyway?"I wanted to know, and so would my readers.

Very few runners—win, lose or draw—are interested in chatting with reporters after spilling their guts along 10,000 meters of cross-country terrain. Rono was scooted away by his coach, John Chaplin, a man not gifted with tact.

"Don't say anything," Rono was instructed, as though a grand jury had just indicted him.

"Bullshit!" I muttered. My tact is not always evident, either.

I figured I'd corner Rono a bit later. I ran over to Illinois' Craig Virgin, who finished third behind Rono and his African teammate, Samson Kimombwa. Virgin, an affable athlete, was under heavy emotional pressure as the defending champion and, in the minds of some, The Great White Hope vs. the Kenyans. Craig had run an outstanding race—as fine a race as one could expect from the young man—but was clearly defeated. Thereupon I confronted him, intruding on his introspection, ready to document for all the world what he would call his failure.

Quite appropriately, he countered, "Right now, I'd just like to sit down and think about this, if you don't mind, mister."

Okay, I pursued other athletes and some coaches, and conducted brief interviews, then returned to Rono and Virgin a bit later, finding both more agreeable. After the complete results were distributed, I hurriedly wrote and filed my stories, sped my rented car 40 miles south to Dallas and just caught my flight before it departed for New York. I was glad I had watched this one—and still covered it adequately. Besides, the thought of investing in a trip to Texas, and not viewing the race, was disconcerting.

People watch cross-country for different reasons. Some folks do it by accident. They view the herds of runners with amusement as they stroll through the park. Then, there are the coaches, officials, parents, teammates, reporters and photographers, and general fans, each with his defined mission. How well they are able to enjoy the reaces will depend upon their allegiance to these time-honored principles:

1. Know the Course. If your know the specific route, you can plan your position at given points for optimal viewing. You can also judge whether you can negotiate the tougher terrain that must be followed to gain a special vantage point. Moreover, if, for example, you know that there is a descent in the latter part of the course, you may be wise to be close to the finish—otherwise, you will not see it—with a mile or so to go.

At a national championship meet, which attracts running addicts from near and far, there is usually a high degree of unfamiliarity with the course among spectators. This was apparent at the 1976 AAU run at Philadelphia's Fairmount Park. It is a rather hilly route and many onlookers, no doubt runners included, were frantic with bewilderment as they tried to plot their positions. I was among them.

2. Establish Priorities. You cannot dance at every party, and you cannot see the entire race. If you attempt the impossible, you might end up with nothing. What is important to you? A scenic part of the course? A certain runner? The dramatic finish? Don't spread yourself too thin. You may have to give up seeing the finish in order to enjoy other parts of the race. At many sites, it is difficult to do both.

3. Equip Yourself. Coaches have to bring everything but the kitchen sink. A wristwatch and stopwatch are important, not so much to time the runners as to gauge when they will pass through certain spots. If you're stationed at the two-mile mark in a college race and you note 10 minutes have gone by, get ready. . . because here they come. Of course, it does not hurt to know that a runner is on record pace with a mile to go. A good pair of binoculars is invaluable for obvious reasons. A map of the course and a meet program or entry list will also help.

4. Get High. High up, that is. Common sense tells you you'll see better that way. Find a hill or rock or bench—anything that will put you above the level of the runners. How frustrating it is to have to get up on your toes and stretch your neck to catch a glimpse of the action.

5. Use Ingenuity. It sometimes requires a lot of cleverness, even some of that old grade-school mischief, to get a good look. The impossible can become possible with the proper ingenuity and, well, madness.

Find a sturdy tree limb, and with field glasses you'll have the view of the crow's nest. You will also be relied upon by people around you to alert them to the appearance of oncoming runners. Take turns going piggyback on your friend's shoulders. Compact, foldout stools, positioned on high, level ground, will work.

A motorized cart is a dream on a golf course. These carts are used by key officials. If you are acquainted with these people and volunteer to help in some way, perhaps you can talk your way into a lift during the race. If you live nearby, bring your own, but be discreet and very prudent—and don't tell anyone *I* told you to do so. Then there is my fantasy of renting a helicopter and following the runners for the entire run. This is selfish because of the noise, but fantasies are supposed to be selfish.

6. Forget the Start. If you insist on being there for the gun, the field may escape you on the meat of the course. Some routes are designed in such a way so that the start and finish, and other parts of the course are all situated in one area. This is convenient, and in such cases the vicinity of the start is the place to be.

7. Think Colors. In order to keep tabs on contending teams, it is easier to isolate uniform colors than the names printed on them, or even to spot familiar faces in the field. Some uniforms only carry the team nickname (e.g., Bruisers). While you are discerning them, the field will already be at your next checkpoint. However, if five teams of equal ability are wearing navy blue and white, the color system will break down.

If your concentrate on colors and can think quickly, you can determine, for example, that Team A, the favorite, wearing brown stripes, is in deep trouble after four miles because its fifth man was struggling in the back on the pack.

For the really shrewd operators, there is the opportunity to make like a cop estimating crowd size at marches and parades. Police officials can determine that 10,000 persons watched a parade by computing the density of persons in a given space and considering the total area of the activity. At a cross-country meet you can estimate, say, that runners will move six abreast through a certain spot on the course. You then "eyeball" what appears to be about a 50-yard stretch and figure that in a dense pack there might be roughly 20 "rows" of runners in those 50 yards, or about 120 runners.

Back to the color system. You're keying on Team Z, your alma mater, and Team X, its fiercest rival. By quickly noting how spread out these teams' runners are, you can calculate their approximate point totals and move on to your next vantage point. This takes longer to explain than it does to compute, and it is only for the hard core.

Sometimes, a meet employs a unique system that forces the spectator to realign his approach. There is a high school meet in New York called the State Intersectional. It brings together harriers from every part of the state—except New York City. It is a prelude to the ensuing state championship, which includes the city. The state is divided into 11 geographical sections, and scoring is done on that basis as well as for individual teams.

The runners do not wear their usual team shirts; they are outfitted by section. For example, contestants from Section Two, the Albany area, wear maroon shirts lettered only with "Section 2," even though they may represent 50 different schools. The sectional scoring is relatively insignificant. The team results are weighed quite heavily as athletes peak for this meet. But the color system makes it next to impossible to gauge the team contenders during the race. The sectional colors are: baby blue, maroon, gold, scarlet, violet, orange, green, royal blue, white and navy blue. (Yes, that's only 10—one of the sections does not compete in cross-country.) This is a photographer's delight if he's shooting color but a spectator's nightmare. Who's who? Who knows?

8. Don't Rough It. How many times have I sworn at myself for not bringing that extra sweater on a "pleasant" October day? Those who arrive with turtlenecks, gloves and hooded windbreakers become the envy of the rest of us, who are clad more to run than watch. Spectators in Baton Rouge do not have the worries of those in Boston.

If you spent a day in the park with your family or by yourself with an absorbing novel or the Sunday papers, you'd prepare yourself with a lunch, a radio, sun lotion and whatnot. The whatnot is also needed at a cross-country meet which, in many place, is situated miles away from the nearest mandatory services.

9. **Show Courtesy.** Don't crowd the runners. Give them room. Cooperate with the officials. Don't litter the course. Cheer *all* of the harriers. If you're calling off split times, be accurate so as not to inadvertently mislead the runners. And please do not ridicule the lagging runners. To do so is to bring down yourself.

These are not rules to memorize but hints to consider as they apply. Common sense and common decency work well. Cross-country can be fun to watch, but when everyone's gone and the flags have been rolled up, take a trip on the running course and add an appropriate ending to a perfect day.

References

Periodicals

The Harrier, Marc Bloom, editor & publisher. (Staten Island, N.Y.)

Met Track, John Homlish and Tom Donlon, editors. (New York, N.Y.)

Runner's World, Bob Anderson, publisher; Joe Henderson, editor. (Mountain View, Calif.)

Track & Field News, Bert Nelson, editor & publisher. (Los Altos, Calif.)

Books

Always Young, by Frank Dolson. World Publications (Mountain View, Calif.), 1975.

Athletics and Football, by Montague Shearman. Longmans, Green and Company (London), 1887.

Athletics of Today, by F.A.M. Webster. Frederick Warne & Co. (London and New York), 1929.

Distance and Cross-Country Running, by George Orton. American Sports Publishing Co. (New York, N.Y.), 1903.

Dr. Sheehan on Running, by Dr. George Sheehan. World Publications (Mountain View, Calif.), 1975.

The Gerry Lindgren Story, compiled by Jim Dunne. World Publications (Mountain View, Calif.), 1971.

History Preserved—A Guide to New York City Landmarks and Historic Districts, by Harmon H. Goldstone and Martha Dalrymple. Schocken Books (New York), 1976.

International Amateur Athletics Federation Handbook. The IAAF (London), 1977.

National College Athletic Association Track & Field Guide. NCAA Publishing Service (Shawnee Mission, Kans.), 1977.

National Federation Track & Field Rules & Records, Clifford B. Fagan, editor. National Federation of State High School Athletic Associations (Elgin, Ill.), 1977.

Olympic Track & Field, Bert Nelson, editor. Tafnews Press (Los Altos, Calif.), 1975.

The Realm of Sport, Herbert Warren Wind, editor. Simon & Schuster (New York), 1966.

Running and Cross-Country Running, by Afred Shrubb. Health and Strength, Ltd. (London), c. 1910.

Runner's Training Guide, Joe Henderson, editor, World Publications (Mountain View, Calif.), 1973.

The Self-Made Olympian, by Ron Daws. World Publications (Mountain View, Calif.), 1977.

The Frank Shorter Story, by John Parker. World Publications (Mountain View, Calif.), 1972.

Sportsource, Bob Anderson, editor. World Publications (Mountain View, Calif.), 1975.

Teenage Distance Running, by Kim Valentine. Tafnews Press (Los Altos, Calif.), 1973.

Van Aaken Method, by Ernst van Aaken, M.D. World Publications (Mountain View, Calif.), 1976.

The Varied World of Cross-Country, Joe Henderson, editor. (World Publications (Mountain View, Calif.), 1972.

Index

About the Author

Marc Bloom has lived all of his 30 years in New York City and was graduated from the City College of New York in 1969. He teaches language arts and creative writing in a Queens junior high school.

Since 1966, Bloom has also been a free-lance writer and editor and has contributed articles to many publications including *The New York Times, Long Island Press, Sports Digest, Boys' Life, Letterman, Track & Field News* and *Runner's World.* He began publishing *The Harrier* in 1974.

Bloom has been intimately involved in the promotion of runners and running for many years, and in 1975 received the Public Schools Athletic League Coaches Association of New York Community Service Award "for outstanding service to the youth of our city and to our city community."

Bloom has seen hundreds of cross-country races in the last 15 years and has been running almost daily himself since 1972. In 1976, he completed the New York City Marathon in 3:17.

He now lives on Staten Island with his wife Andrea and their four-year-old daughter, Allison.